Ela! Ela!

Come! Come!

I acknowledge the traditional owners of the land on which this book was made: the Wurundjeri Woi Wurrung people of the Kulin Nation. Sovereignty has never been ceded; I pay my respects to Elders past and present.

Ela! Ela!

To Turkey and Greece, a journey home through food

Ella Mittas

murdoch books

Sydney | London

Introduction

My father's side of the family is Greek. They all live on one street, in houses next door to each other. There are holes cut between backyard fences, so everyone can be together easily. That one small section of street has given me a sense of community and belonging I haven't been able to locate in the rest of my life. It seems separate from the rest of Australia, but it's a version of Greece abstracted from the real thing; its traditions are built on distant memories. The language spoken is Gringlish, a mix of both places. I've always felt that somewhere inside that place, among the carved-out fences, is where my true identity lies. I've looked for more concrete examples of that elusive sense of community for years: a place where it exists in its entirety, where it's set in stone.

This collection of essays and recipes is taken from some sort of journey of knowledge. Of food, culture and belonging. In Melbourne, I'd worked under a chef who'd cooked traditional Turkish cuisine and had seen how interwoven it was with Greek food culture. There was even a genre of cuisine in Greece dedicated to the crossover. Politiki Kouzina translates to 'food of the city' and came to Greece from Istanbul via the ethnic Greeks deported from Turkey during the 1923 population exchange. Once I decided I wanted to work in Greece, had applied for my citizenship and was waiting for it to be processed, I thought Istanbul would be the next best thing and chose to wait there.

Where I got the arrogance to believe I'd be accepted in Turkey with no knowledge of the culture is beyond me. I'll put it down to my age and naivety mixed with various forms of privilege. These things helped form my almost willful misunderstanding of how language and culture barriers would affect me anywhere I went and cooked—something glaringly obvious when writing in retrospect, but indecipherable at the time.

I hope you enjoy the stories and recipes in this book. The recipes are a mix of things I saw, ate and was taught. Years of cooking them have turned them into something more my own. But I'd like to thank everyone I worked with nonetheless—mostly for putting up with me. Thanks to my family and friends for that, too. I would write out a thousand thank yous but I would prefer to say that my own community I've built and am continuing to build is everything and the reason I ever cooked at all.

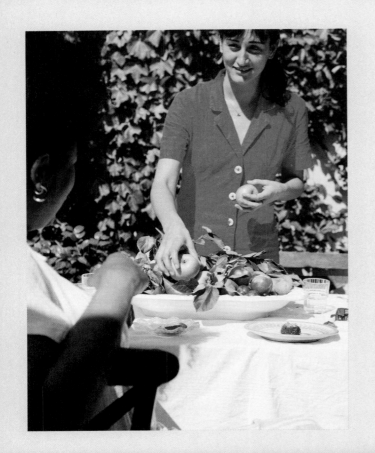

Contents

1. Istanbul

I arrived in Istanbul at the peak of summer. I'd picked out an apartment to live in, almost at random, from a tiny thumbnail image on a website. It was in Tarlabaşı, an area whose name elicited a mix of surprise and concern from people when I mentioned it. The buildings there were dilapidated in a way that made it seem like they were leaning in to touch each other. Ropes of washing hung through windows and off balconies, tying them together. I'd walk underneath them on my way to Istiklal, the city's main promenade.

As I'd walk, the air would be permeated with the smell of chicken pilaf from the street food vendors who'd wait on each corner. Baklava gleamed at me, dripping with syrup from brightly lit shopfronts. I'd walk through crowds until I was overwhelmed. I'd take the ferry across the Bosphorus from Europe to Asia if I had time. I'd cue Brian Eno's "The Big Ship", to perfectly match the sunset as I crossed continents. That journey never felt less surreal.

Nights in Tarlabaşı were unbearably loud, but when I closed the window in my carpeted room the air in it would turn thick with heat. Wide-eyed and wide awake, I'd listen to the men who sat on the stoop in front of my window to watch YouTube videos together and chain-smoke. Initially, I was grateful I couldn't understand Turkish, that the sound would partially wash over me.

The elderly couple who owned the building lived on the floor above me. Fatma told me I could call her Anne: "Mum". Hassan, her husband, would mostly shake his head and laugh when he saw me. He'd "tsk tsk tsk" me, wagging his finger in my face, for forgetting to water the plants in my windowsill, or for coming home late. He'd knock at my door and say, "Be careful

10—41

at night," and I'd think, Okay, okay, I'm not a kid. But one evening walking home, I was stopped by policemen with guns and bulletproof vests. A car had been torched outside a bar near my apartment and the street was blocked off. As I stood there watching the flames in the midnight air, I imagined being safe in bed. Police were moving with urgency, bystanders were yelling at them, and I couldn't decipher anything. When I was finally let past the barricades, walking home through the night, all I could think about was how little I knew about where I was.

The restaurant I'd organised to work in was in the waterfront suburb of Karaköy. The food was contemporary Turkish with a short, revolving menu of seasonal dishes— a concept relatively new to Turkey at the time. At work, the boys didn't know what to think of me. They'd call each other *kanka* or *abi*, but for me, they'd just whistle. Sometimes they'd stand together and watch me work. They'd take turns showing me googled photos of the Melbourne skyline on their phones and I'd nod.

My head chef sat on a stool, either in the corner of the kitchen with the boys congregated around him, or out the front of the restaurant smoking. If there was something I needed to ask him, I had to approach him, and wait for him to address me. He wasn't often busy; just sitting and doing nothing, not quite ready to answer.

"Chef?" I'd wait, and he'd stare off into the distance.

We liked each other but fought. I didn't understand his cooking methods, and looking back I didn't try to. I thought the way he cooked was all based on myth. He told me honey had too much energy. That if you gave too much to people, they'd go crazy. For that reason, the honey syrup dessert we made had only a cup of honey in it and was topped up with kilos of pure white sugar, instead. He tried to make me change how I caramelised onions; his way was to burn them, then pour water over them to deglaze the pan. I argued that his onions wouldn't be as sweet as mine, that the colour he was getting didn't equal flavour. He argued it was his kitchen and his rules, and if I didn't like it, I could leave.

He did concede to let me put dessert specials on if I finished all my regular work, though. A small piece of control to keep me occupied. I'd finish everything as fast as I could to put complicated French-style pastries on the specials board. Everyone would sit down for an extended breakfast: boiled eggs, cucumber, tomato, olives, feta, simit, olive oil, tea and cigarettes, and I'd be alone, working as hard as I could. Just me and the white noise of the extraction fan.

Another chef that worked on my shift was Deniz. He was big and broad with paws for hands that looked disconnected from his body when he used them. I'd hoped we would get along because he had lived in Australia and spoke English. I'd stand next to him telling him all the things I loved about home, what I missed. But the more I talked, the more annoyed he'd get. He said he loved Australia and wished he could've stayed. So I stopped talking to him about it.

The first thing Deniz did in the mornings was make himself a Turkish coffee. He'd then drag a chair to the middle of the back room and sit, legs stretched out, one hand balancing the tiny cup on his stomach, the other arm hanging limply near the ground. He'd sit like that with his eyes glazed over—sometimes for hours. I couldn't believe how little he worked; I would stand in the doorway, watching him, thinking if he were in Australia he'd be fired.

In my room at night, I sat on my bed and attempted to learn Turkish. I cut pieces of cardboard into squares to make flashcards that littered my floor. I downloaded a translating app for my phone that I could speak into and went through all the things I could remember the boys saying to me during the day, sounding the words out phonetically. I'd say "*Gerizekalı*" into it, and it would read the translation back at me: "Idiot".

Deniz refused to help me translate things. He pretended not to hear me when I'd say things needed to be ordered. He would freeze, and his eyes would get wide, like he was focusing all his power on making me disappear. He'd watch me putting Post-its around the kitchen with lists I'd tried to write in Turkish. I'd pin copies in everyone's sections, point at them, saying, "This is my vegetable order, okay?" I'd show the young boy who worked on my section, too. He spoke some English, but only bothered to translate a list of insults he wrote in my notebook. I'd try to mime the things we needed to the boy, who pretended he couldn't see me. Deniz would stand behind him, avoiding eye contact so hard that he'd almost look lobotomised. By the time I left the restaurant each day, I felt like I didn't exist. In the mornings, I'd get back to work, and nothing I'd ordered would have come.

The boys preferred more traditional Turkish sweets to the elaborate, involved ones I'd make. They'd eat my desserts with expressions of indifference, which sometimes felt out of spite. My chef would laugh, shrug, and tell me my desserts were, "Fine."

Somewhere six months in was when the deep feeling of isolation set in. Basic communication had been the hardest thing at first, but once I learnt the Turkish words for numbers, foods and the recipes I had to read, I spent most of my days working in silence. I was used to being under extreme time pressure at home, but productivity was viewed differently here. There was so much time left in the day, even with all my tricks of the extra work I was creating. Extra time that was filled with nothing, seeing as I couldn't really communicate.

Kitchens are set up as hierarchies: you graduate through sections as you spend more time in a job. New sections come with the new knowledge it takes to master each section. The lowest section was mine: cold dishes. The most senior rung in our kitchen was on the pans, where Deniz worked: the hot section. I decided I wanted to learn his position. I fixated on him during service, trying to memorise his movements. Which seasoning he used for what; his timing; his flourishes. My chef hung the potential of moving to the hot section over my head indefinitely. The only way to get there, I concluded after tirelessly asking, was to offer to work for free, outside of my roster. My chef laughed from his stool in the corner when I arrived for my volunteer night shift. My teacher, Deniz, didn't acknowledge me as I sidled up next to him on the hot section.

Orders started coming through, slowly to start, so I danced behind Deniz, who managed to keep me blocked off, hiding nearly everything he did. Dockets started spitting out of the ticket machine and Deniz began moving faster. I waited for him to explain anything to me, but his back continued to face me like a giant barricade. Every step I tried to take forward, it pushed me back in place. As Deniz knocked me out of the way once again, I said to him, "Deniz, are you going to let me touch anything?"

At first I thought he didn't hear me. But when I asked again, he threw his tongs down, turned and abandoned me. In front of me every burner was alight.

I knew I couldn't manage it. Things were burning but I had to step back.

Slowly Deniz came over and took control again. I approached my chef in his corner and said, "If I come again, will it be like this?"

He laughed. "This is not a school for you. We are not teachers." And in a flash I understood that what I was pushing for wasn't on offer.

Initially, all I felt was confusion and betrayal after that night. I couldn't understand the withholding of knowledge. With time, though, came the clarity of how unrealistic I'd been about my dynamic in the kitchen, and how frustrated I'd been with being made to feel uncomfortable. How entitled that was. Until then, in my mind, culture shock had been exotic-looking objects shining at me too brightly. It took me a while to realise I was having culture shock all the time.

Shallow-Fried Eggplant

You can make this eggplant a few hours before serving to let it steep in the marinade. It's great as a side or excellent as a starter on grilled bread. I sometimes serve it with goat's cheese too—although I didn't include that in the recipe because I don't think it's very Turkish. Depending on the season I garnish this dish with either the tomato mix or pomegranate. I don't think there's too much use in salting eggplants nowadays to get rid of the bitterness; it's mostly been bred out of them. But I have found salting them and introducing them to some oil before frying helps them to absorb less once they're in the pan. I mostly use olive oil from Crete because I love its grassy flavour, but any other extra virgin olive oil will work perfectly.

Serves 4 as a side

2 large eggplants (aubergines)
canola oil
flake salt to season

For the marinade:
½ cup (125 ml) red
    wine vinegar
1 clove garlic, sliced
1 tbsp honey
2 tbsp extra virgin olive oil
2 tbsp lemon juice
2 tbsp parsley, chopped
flake salt and freshly ground
    black pepper to taste

For the garnish:
3 tomatoes, diced
½ red onion, diced
2 tbsp extra virgin olive oil
2 tbsp lemon juice
flake salt and freshly ground
    black pepper to taste

Or:
½ cup (90 g) pomegranate
    seeds
mint

1. Start by peeling the eggplants. I peel mine lengthways in stripes, leaving 2-cm (¾-in) strips of skin in between (this striped effect looks great and also makes the eggplant easier to eat). Then cut into rounds about 1½–2 cm (⅝–¾ in) thick.

2. Once cut, lightly salt the eggplant and douse in around 3 tablespoons oil and leave to one side for 5 or so minutes to marinate.

3. Heat 2 cm (¾ in) of canola oil in a frypan over a medium heat.

4. Shallow-fry the eggplant slices until very golden; you'll need to keep topping up the oil as it's absorbed.

5. Once the eggplant is cooked, drain on a paper towel to get rid of excess oil.

6. Arrange on a serving dish and season with salt. I arrange mine in circles that follow the line on the plate I'm serving on and spiral in.

7. Mix the marinade ingredients well, then pour over the eggplant slices.

8. Combine garnish ingredients and arrange over the eggplant, or sprinkle with the pomegranate seeds and mint. Best served still slightly warm.

Mücver

These zucchini fritters are based on a recipe from the restaurant. Because we made them in such large batches, it'd take one person an entire day to prepare the mix: grating kilos of zucchini, salting them and squeezing out all the water. It is essential to get as much liquid out of the zucchinis as possible, even though it's time-consuming. Your fritters will end up crispier and tastier, so take your time. Aleppo pepper is a variety of capsicum that's dried, crushed and used as a spice. It's mildly spicy, with some fruitiness and cumin-like undertones, and is a brilliant red. It's easily found at Middle Eastern grocers but can be substituted with a mix of smoked paprika and cayenne pepper.

Serves 4 as a starter

2 large zucchini (courgettes), grated
4 spring onions (scallions), chopped
100 g (3½ oz) feta
1 cup (40–60 g) chopped mixed dill, mint and parsley
¾ cup (110 g) flour
2 eggs

Aleppo pepper to taste
vegetable oil for deep frying
flake salt, freshly ground black pepper and lemon to taste

1. Mix the grated zucchini with 1 tablespoon of salt and leave it to drain in a colander for 10 minutes. Rinse the mix then hand-squeeze out as much water as possible. The fritters will be too wet if not enough moisture is taken out.

2. Mix the squeezed-out zucchini with the spring onions, feta, herbs, Aleppo pepper and lemon. Taste to check the seasoning, then add the flour and eggs. Mix together thoroughly: it will be a fairly wet dough but should be firm enough to keep shape if scooped up in a spoonful. Usually, I check the density of my fritters by frying one and seeing if it holds together. Add a little more flour if necessary.

3. Heat oil for deep-frying until it's hot enough to drop some of the mix in and have it brown in 30 seconds. Turn the heat down to medium. Using a dessert spoon, carefully drop scoops of the mix into the hot oil. Do this in batches. Cook for 1½ minutes until golden brown and cooked through. You should be able to make 15–16 fritters. Remove with a slotted spoon and drain on paper towels.

Kısır—Ruby Bulgur Salad

This salad is great in summer straight out of the fridge. Salça is a Turkish paste made from salted capsicums. It adds great richness to dishes, but you can leave it out if you can't get your hands on any.

Serves 4 as a side

1 small beetroot
⅓ cup (80 ml) extra virgin olive oil
2 cups (350 g) fine bulgur
2 cups (500 ml) boiling water
2 Lebanese (short) cucumbers
1 tbsp Turkish sweet red pepper paste (biber salcasi; available from Middle Eastern grocers)
½ cup (10 g) parsley, chopped
½ cup (10 g) mint, chopped
½ cup (80 g) smoked almonds, roughly chopped
¼ cup (60 ml) pomegranate molasses
1 lemon, juiced

flake salt and freshly ground black pepper to taste

1. Start by boiling the beetroot until very tender. I do this with the skin on. Once the beetroot is cooked all the way through, you should be able to wipe the skin off.

2. Blend the beetroot in a food processor until very smooth. Add some of the olive oil to make the blending easier if you need.

3. Put the bulgur in a bowl. Then pour the boiling water over it and give it a quick stir before covering with a lid or cling wrap and set aside.

4. While the bulgur is absorbing water, dice the cucumbers into cubes of around 1 cm (½ in).

5. Once the bulgur has softened, work the pepper paste and beetroot through with your hands, making sure it gets spread through the mix evenly.

6. Then stir through the herbs, nuts and cucumber, then season with pomegranate molasses, lemon, pepper paste, olive oil, salt and pepper.

Chicken Rice

This is my take on the chicken pilaf we'd buy from street vendors on our way home after nights out. It was the best part of going for a drink. The street food was my highlight of living in the city—buying roasted chestnuts in the snow; going to get a morning simit, a ring-shaped bread covered in sesame, served wrapped in newspaper—always such a treat, always such an event. This dish is best served on the day of making it.

Serves 6

To poach the chicken:
3 chicken marylands
6 cups (1.5 litre) water
table salt

For the pilaf:
¼ cup (35 g) slivered almonds
4 tbsp butter
3 cups (600 g) aged
    basmati rice
1 brown onion, diced
2 tsp cinnamon
5 cups (1.25 litres) chicken
    stock, from the poaching
2 tbsp lemon juice
¼ cup (5 g) parsley, chopped

flake salt to taste

1. Start by placing the chicken marylands in a pot and cover them with water. You want to use around 6 cups (1 litre), so choose a pot that will allow them to be submerged with that volume of liquid.

2. Salt the water with 2 tablespoons of table salt, bring up to a boil, then turn down to a soft simmer.

3. Cook until just past pink, around 25–30 minutes, then take off the heat, leaving the chicken to continue cooking in the hot liquid.

4. Once the stock is cooled, put to one side and shred the chicken.

5. Fry off the almonds in 1 tablespoon of the butter over low heat until golden. Then drain on a paper towel to get rid of excess butter. Leave to one side.

6. Soak rice in cold water for 20 minutes, then drain well.

7. Put a large frying pan on medium heat and add 1 tablespoon butter. Once it's melted, add the onion, cinnamon and a pinch of salt. Cook until the onions are caramelised: 15–20 minutes.

8. Add the drained rice and fry off until well coated in butter. While you're doing this, bring the stock up to the boil in another pot.

9. Slowly add 3 cups (750 ml) of stock to the rice, bringing the liquid up to a soft simmer. Cover with a lid and cook until the stock is absorbed, checking every couple of minutes.

10. Add remaining stock in increments, checking rice as you go.

11. Once the rice is cooked through (this will take 15–20 minutes), take off the heat and leave to steam for 5 minutes, with the lid on.

12. Stir through shredded chicken, the remaining 2 tablespoons butter, lemon juice and chopped parsley, and check for seasoning.

13. Serve immediately, garnished with almonds.

Cauliflower Freekeh Salad

You can use the pilaf base of this salad with any vegetable combination. Sometimes I use roast carrots and red grapes instead of cauliflower or serve the base plain with currants and almonds stirred through. If you don't have any stock, you can cook the freekeh in water—it just won't be as rich.

Serves 6 as a side

2 heads cauliflower,
  broken into florets
4 tbsp extra virgin olive oil,
  plus extra to finish
1 brown onion, diced
1 tbsp butter
2 cups (400 g) freekeh
2 cups (500 ml) hot vegetable
  or chicken stock
1 cup (40–60 g) chopped
  mixed parsley, mint, dill and
  spring onion (scallion)
¼ cup (35 g) chopped
  hazelnuts, roasted

flake salt, freshly ground black
  pepper and lemon to taste

Dressing:
½ cup (130 g) Greek yoghurt
½ lemon, juiced
½ garlic clove, crushed
1 tbsp tahini

flake salt to taste

1. Preheat oven to 200°C (400°F). Toss the cauliflower in 3 tablespoons of olive oil and season with salt and pepper. Bake for around 30 minutes or until golden brown, and set aside to cool.

2. Place the onion, butter and 1 tablespoon of olive oil in a large heavy-based pot and sauté on medium heat for 15–20 minutes, until the onion is golden brown.

3. Add the freekeh to the onion and fry out until it's all coated in oil.

4. Add the hot stock and stir well. Be careful when you do this: sometimes the stock can spit.

5. Bring liquid to the boil, then reduce the heat to low and leave to simmer for 15 minutes with the lid on. I check on the pilaf a couple of times throughout this cooking process, to see if the mix has dried out.

6. Once the freekeh is cooked through, remove from the heat and aerate it by running a fork through it to fluff it up. Then leave to cool slightly.

7. Meanwhile, mix the yoghurt with lemon juice, garlic and tahini, and season.

8. Then stir the mixed greens and cauliflower into the pilaf and adjust seasoning. Add more olive oil if it's a little dry.

9. Spoon into a serving dish and garnish with dressing and roast hazelnuts.

Istanbul

Slow-Cooked Lamb Shoulder

I shred this lamb after cooking and serve it on top of the flatbread garnished with the salad and yoghurt. If you don't have enough time to wait around all day, you can raise the oven temperature to 160°C (315°F) and cook the shoulder for around three hours—the results will still be very good.

Serves 6

1 lamb shoulder, on the bone
6 tbsp smoked paprika
1 tbsp ground cumin
½ tbsp ground coriander
2 sprigs rosemary,
　finely chopped
1 tsp flake salt
4 tbsp extra virgin olive oil
3 cups (750 ml) white wine

flake salt and lemon to taste

1. Preheat oven to 110°C (225°F). Remove the lamb from the fridge and place it into a baking tray, and set aside to come to room temperature.

2. Mix the paprika, cumin, coriander, rosemary and salt in a bowl, pouring in enough olive oil to form a thick paste. Rub the shoulder with the mix.

3. Pour the wine into the baking tray, then cover with baking paper, then foil.

4. Place into the oven and cook for around 8 hours, or until the lamb easily comes away from the bone.

5. Remove from the oven and allow to rest for 20 minutes before serving. Season with salt and lemon before you do so.

For the tahini yoghurt:
1 cup (260 g) yoghurt
2 tbsp tahini
2 tbsp lemon juice
3 tbsp extra virgin olive oil
1 clove garlic, minced

flake salt

1. Leave the yoghurt to strain overnight in a colander lined with cheesecloth (muslin), paper towel or any fabric that will allow for water to drain through.

2. Then, combine the rest of the ingredients, checking for seasoning.

For the sumac onions:
1 red onion, finely sliced
1 tsp sumac
½ cup (10 g) parsley, chopped
2 tbsp lemon juice
3 tbsp extra virgin olive oil

flake salt and freshly ground
　black pepper

1. Put the onion into a bowl with a few pinches of salt and the sumac, and massage ingredients together. This helps the onions to break down slightly. Leave to rest for 5 minutes.

2. Mix through the rest of the garnish ingredients, then you're ready to serve.

For the yoghurt flatbread:
8 cups (1.2 kg) flour
2 tsp yeast
1 tbsp caster sugar
1 tsp flake salt
1½ cups (375 ml) water
1½ cups (390 g) yoghurt
2 tbsp extra virgin olive oil

For grilling:
¼ cup (60 ml) extra virgin
    olive oil
1 clove garlic, grated

flake salt to season

1. Add your dry ingredients to a bowl, creating a well in the middle.

2. Combine your wet ingredients and mix them well before pouring them into the well.

3. Starting from the centre of the well, gradually start to incorporate the flour into the wet ingredients. When everything is combined, turn out onto a lightly floured surface and knead until the dough is smooth and elastic: around 5 minutes.

4. Place dough into a bowl and cover with cling wrap or a clean tea towel and let rise for around 3 hours or until the dough has doubled in size.

5. Once the dough has risen, turn out onto a lightly floured surface and divide into 10 balls.

6. Using a rolling pin, roll each ball out to roughly the size of a dinner plate.

7. Heat a griddle pan over high heat, and combine the oil, garlic and salt.

8. Brush each flatbread lightly with the oil, and grill. Each side will only take 30 seconds or so. This can also be done on the barbecue. Sometimes I cook these flatbreads underneath the spit, letting the fat drip onto them.

9. Once grilled, cover with a tea towel to keep warm until serving.

Braised Leeks with Orange

In the restaurant, we'd get huge crates of seasonal vegetables delivered every morning. One of my jobs was to make meze with whatever came—a daily embodiment of the saying, "What grows together goes together." By the end of the season, once we'd run out of variations on a theme, the results became a bit odd. But this was one of my favourites. These leeks are surprisingly flavourful for how few ingredients are in them. The orange juice cooks down to make almost a glaze that is sweet but bright—great next to fish or as part of a meze spread. I used a small bunch of baby leeks for this recipe, but regular leeks will work just fine.

Serves 4 as a side

2 onions, sliced
4 tbsp extra virgin olive oil
1 clove garlic, sliced
small bunch baby leeks,
    halved horizontally or
    4 large leeks, sliced on
    an angle
1 cup (250 ml) orange juice

flake salt and freshly ground
    black pepper to taste

a few sprigs of dill or mint
    to serve

1. In a large saucepan over medium heat, sauté onions in olive oil until deep golden brown; this will take around 15–20 minutes.

2. Add garlic and sauté for around 30 seconds.

3. Then add the sliced leek and sauté for 3 minutes, until the leeks are covered in oil and have changed colour slightly.

4. Add orange juice, turn down the heat to a low simmer and cover the leeks with either a lid or a cartouche (a layer of baking paper lightly pressed onto the surface of the ingredients). From here, the leeks will take around 15–20 minutes to cook through.

5. Season with salt and pepper. Cool slightly, and serve at room temperature garnished with fresh herbs.

Istanbul

Semolina Halva Irmik Helvas

In Greece, they make this dessert with sweet wine instead of milk and eggs and serve it in the period of Lent when people can't eat animal products. I prefer this version, though, for its richness. Serve warm with ice cream.

Serves 8

250 g (9 oz) fine semolina
1 tsp ground aniseed
140 g (5 oz) butter
500 ml (17 fl oz) milk, plus
   a splash more to beat
   the egg yolks
200 g (7 oz) caster sugar
1 orange, zested
2 egg yolks

roasted almonds to serve

1. Fry off the semolina and ground aniseed in butter until well browned.

2. While this is happening, in another pot bring milk, sugar and orange zest to the boil.

3. Once the semolina is nice and brown, around 15 minutes, take off the heat.

4. Beat the egg yolks with some cold milk in a bowl, then gradually start to temper the egg mix, adding ladles of hot milk to the mix while whisking. Incorporate the hot milk slowly, or the egg yolks will scramble.

5. Once all the milk is integrated into the egg mix, put the semolina back on the stove to bring up to heat.

6. Then combine the milk mix with the semolina, stirring to avoid lumps. As soon as the milk looks close to being absorbed, take off the heat.

7. Serve warm with ice cream and roasted almonds.

2. Alaçatı

When I walked through the streets of Istanbul, each food vendor I passed was an embodied reminder of a dish I hadn't yet learnt: chicken pilaf, *çiğ köfte*, *kokoreç*. I wasn't ready to leave Turkey, but I wanted to relocate. I'd sit in my room at night, trawling through each region of the country's culinary specialities. Gaziantep was the best place to learn about baklava as it was where the pistachios of the country were grown. Izmir was important in the population exchange with Greece, and the food there was where the two cultures met; stuffed capsicums, sarma, olive oil-laden vegetable braises. When I googled "wild weeds of Turkey", among my search results was the Alaçatı Ot Festivali: a festival focused on foraged weeds on the Aegean coast, close to Izmir. The more I read into Alaçatı and that coastline, the more fixated I became. I looked for restaurants in the area obsessively, and Babushka was what I found.

Babushka was run by a woman named Olga, a Russian who'd come to Turkey on a holiday, had fallen in love and stayed. She ran the restaurant with her now husband, Ozgur, and wrote a blog about the traditional Turkish foods she'd learnt to make—this was how I'd found her. On the bus ride there, I tried to think of Istanbul like it had been a practice run. I ran through the mistakes I wasn't going to keep on making.

Because of its proximity, and because originally the town was settled by Greeks, Alaçati had a strong Grecian influence in its architecture and food. The houses were traditional white stone with blue detailing. Bougainvillea framed the cobblestone streets. Glass pendants of the evil eye—like the one I wore around my neck—were nailed to doorways. From the main beach, the Greek island of Chios rose out of the sea. It looked close enough to swim to, all encased in clouds, shadowy blue.

42—73

On her blog, Olga appeared to be a rounded, smiley cook (in pictures, she was streaked in flour, grinning) and so I was surprised, when I first saw her surging towards me in Alaçati's town square, to find she was rail-thin. I couldn't tell if she'd seen me, because she regarded me with such coldness. But then she stopped and said a curt hello before swinging back around. I followed after her, my wheelie bag screaming over stones as I dragged it behind me.

We turned down a lane off the main square and reached a door. "Babushka" was painted in bright red on a wooden sign that was nailed in the centre of an assortment of ornamental dolls. Olga pushed it open, saying, "Everyone, this is Ella." Her skirt streamed after her as she disappeared into the restaurant. The courtyard looked exactly like pictures I'd seen: red chequered tablecloths under wooden lattices swelling with grapevines. Four teenage boys were convened around a woman and were singing to her in a mock serenade as traditional music blared from an iPhone. The woman sat there laughing. She was stuffing zucchini flowers with cheese, folding them into neat parcels with one hand, holding a cigarette in the other. They all paused at my arrival, their eyes bouncing between each other. They tentatively smiled and the woman pulled out a chair for me. "*Gel, gel*," she said, and I obeyed, moving over to join them. The woman introduced herself as Gulay Abla, and gestured to the boys saying she was like their mother, that she was like the restaurant's mother. Then the tallest, broadest, loudest boy, Hasan, went about orchestrating introductions from the others. He directed two of the boys to present the matching tattoos they had on their forearms—each consisted of the words "my life" followed by the jagged line of a heart monitor—as a way of explaining they were cousins. The tall, broad one then took me through the restaurant and pointed out all the essentially Turkish things. In the kitchen, he picked up a tray of stuffed capsicums, turned to me, and said, "*Dolma*," followed by making a chef's kiss with his hands and mouth. He swung the fridge open to pull out the clotted cream and tap, tap, tapped on its plastic container, gave me a knowing look and said, "*Kaymak*." We went through the whole fridge before he let me sit back down.

My job at the restaurant was to make and serve meze. The meze were mostly small plates of olive oil-braised vegetables served at room temperature—*zeytinyaği*—or dishes that included wild foraged weeds. Olga's food was bright and fresh. She took pride in the fact that vegetables were the centrepieces of the meals she made, which was how I liked to cook, too.

We would go to the local market together twice a week; my favourite activity in town. At the market there were mountains of greens in piles over plastic sheeting; the foragers sat surrounded by them. Their overflowing baskets were carried straight from the fields. What we found at the market we would integrate through the daily menu. Purslane *(semizotu)*, mixed with strained yoghurt and garlic. Samphire *(deniz börülcesi)*, blanched with its stem pulled out, dressed in olive oil, lemon and garlic. Wild asparagus *(tilkişen)*, sautéed in oil and cooked with eggs. Wild fennel *(arapsaci)* with its sweet anise flavour, stuffed into *börek*. All things I'd never cooked with before.

Preparing meze involved the most time-consuming tasks: processing and washing the greens in big plastic containers in the courtyard; carving out artichoke hearts; cutting beetroots into tiny cubes. Olga was taking my knife off me constantly, brow furrowed. She'd show me how I could cut off more artichoke to get rid of any tough bits, or take off less because throwing away food was "a sin". But her instruction seemed to fluctuate depending on how close to God she was feeling. I admired her dedication to produce, but it frustrated me, too.

I still carried that pressure of time efficiency from home. Her persistent criticism seemed to hint that my attitude had no place in her small home kitchen, though. She'd rather tasks took all day and were done with consideration. I'd never been asked to work more slowly before.

Via email I'd been promised a house to live in as part of my salary. But Olga and her husband Ozgur had so much trouble finding me something that they put me up in the hotel next door, where I was the only guest. The hotel's owner, Yasar, was a short man in his late fifties, who dressed in black pinstriped shirts with heavy gold chain necklaces. I could see my reflection in the Prada sunglasses he wore even when inside.

In the mornings, I woke up to a blinding brightness. My hotel room was furnished in a hundred hues of white. I would watch Yasar through my venetian blinds as he sat smoking in the sun, waiting for me to get up. I'd try to pre-empt his movements and avoid him. But if I did too good a job, he'd knock at my door reeking of *raki*. He'd walk in saying, "Are you fine?" and I'd say, "I'm fine, I'm fine." He'd ask if I wanted him to wash my clothes, if I wanted to have breakfast with him, or if I needed to borrow money. "Anything you need, tell me," he'd say.

I'd try to sneak past him to the beach. Some mornings, I'd notice him trailing behind me on his scooter. I swam further and further out to sea each day. It was the only place I felt I had privacy. Further and further towards Greece, towards that shadowy blue figure that seemed both within reach, and heartbreakingly far.

Each morning, in a display of stoic hospitality, Olga would cook me and Ozgur breakfast at the restaurant. And we'd take part in slightly rearranged versions of the same conversation, the one that centred around Ozgur's nationalistic views.

We'd be eating our *sujuk*, fried eggs and *simit* and he'd say something like, "What do you think of Kurdish people?" and

I'd say, "Well, what do you mean?" He'd say, "A Kurdish person is just a Turkish person, don't you think?" Some mornings he'd only speak to me in Turkish, and when I didn't understand, he'd act annoyed. Occasionally, Yasar would climb the fence, peer down into the courtyard and get Ozgur to translate to me while we ate. Ozgur would say, "He saw you going to the beach today." I'd say, "I know." And Yasar would look at me, shaking his head in disbelief.

In the evenings, it was my job to season all the meze before service. Olga had strict guidelines compiled in a black Moleskine the size of my palm. Every bit of salt, lemon, vinegar was weighed out to the gram, so there was little room for error. I still managed to make mistakes, mainly with garlic. Olga often looked offended when she tasted things I made. Once she spat a mouthful of salad I'd seasoned into the bin, then washed her mouth out like I'd tried to poison her. I stopped using garlic in everything. She could still taste it, she told me.

At night during service the boys would riot around; sometimes they'd fight physically and I'd watch Olga close her eyes, trying to ground herself. She'd drown us out by listening to loops of Buddhist chanting through headphones and we'd have to spend whole services without asking her anything.

If I ever had to go out onto the floor, foreign customers would ask me, "How did you end up here?" and I'd find myself taking a seat to tell them everything that'd happened in the last little while. Ozgur would bring me wine, thinking I was entertaining, as I'd tell them how every night when I went to bed, Ozgur and the boys blasted France Gall's "Ella, Elle l'a" so loudly, that the lyrics
Ella, elle l'a, Ella, elle l'a
would stream into my bedroom and keep me awake. I'd tell them I was pretty sure Olga resented me as much as I resented her: how

one night, mid-service, she made a point of teaching me how to wash my hands in front of everyone and how humiliating it was. I'd take them through the trajectory of our intensifying relationship, and explain how it'd pushed her to want more control over the way I cooked. She wanted control of everything I did, I'd tell them. I'd describe in less detail how I retaliated. As my mood diminished, in the kitchen the boys started saying, "*Kızın nesi var?*" What's wrong with the girl? I stopped trying to humour them.

After the dinner rush, Olga would disappear for the night. Then Gulay Abla and I would sit, drinking tea in silence. She'd force-feed me sweets, pinching my cheeks if I refused. And the boys would perform for us. Arman, the youngest, had a belly shaped like a bowling ball that he'd bounce in time to music. He'd hold a tea towel over his head and the other boys would kneel at his feet, circling him, cheering, looking back at us to see if we were enjoying the show.

Two months passed before I told Olga I didn't want to stay for summer. I said I felt guilty for going but she surprised me and said, "In fifty years from now, do you think you'll regret leaving?" I said, "No." I didn't think I'd even regret it tomorrow. Then she said she understood that she was hard to work with. She said, "I can see how people react to me. It's hard for me too." And I wished I could've managed to be more generous with her.

The next morning, I got a text saying, "Ella, I wish you all the best, you can leave your key with Yasar Abi." I replied, "Thanks for the opportunity Olga, I hope we'll see each other again."

As I drove out to Izmir the next day, the sky was so big. I looked into the rolling mountains, and everything felt epic, and terrifyingly huge. I drove in silence and all I could think was, *Thank God this'll be over soon.*

Alaçatı

Tzatziki with Almonds

This tzatziki is great for using up dregs of herbs you have left over from cooking. Use all the stalks of the herbs in this dish, and the greens of spring onions—it will add to the texture. Very good with chicken souvlaki or any grilled meat.

Serves 6 as a side

500 g (1 lb 2 oz) Greek yoghurt
2 Lebanese (short) cucumbers
3 tbsp extra virgin olive oil
½ cup (20–30 g) chopped mixed dill, mint and spring onion (scallion)
1 clove garlic, minced
1 lemon, juiced
50 g (1¾ oz) roast almonds, crushed

flaked salt and freshly ground black pepper to taste

1. Start by straining the yoghurt overnight through a colander lined with a clean kitchen cloth or some paper towel.

2. The next day, finely dice the cucumber. I do this by cutting four sides off it, leaving the core, then cutting each side lengthways into 1-cm (½-inch) strips, then cutting into 1 cm (½ inch) dice. I find the cores contain too much water, so I eat them as I'm making this. But you can add them in if you prefer.

3. Then mix the rest of your ingredients through and season well. It should be garlicky, lemony, salty and fresh. If you are making this in advance, wait to add the almonds until just before serving, because they will lose their crunch.

Vine Leaf Pesto

This pesto is great mixed through blanched greens or white beans like the ones at the start of my recipes for gigantes with pekmez. You can even combine the two. I make it with the left-over vine leaves I have at the end of making dolmades.

12 brined vine leaves, drained, blanched and trimmed
⅔ cup (170 ml) extra virgin olive oil, or more as needed
1 cup (60 g) parsley, chopped
2 garlic cloves
⅔ cup (100 g) toasted pine nuts or ⅔ cup (110 g) toasted blanched almonds
3 tbsp grape molasses

flaked salt and freshly ground black pepper to taste
1 lemon, juiced

1. Roughly chop the vine leaves and place them in a food processor with a blade attachment. Blitz with a couple of tablespoons of oil until fine.

2. Place the parsley and garlic in the processor and pulse until the mixture is a dense paste.

3. Then add the nuts and pulse until incorporated; I like my pesto to be quite coarse, so I don't like to blend the nuts too much.

4. Then gradually add olive oil and grape molasses until you have the consistency you desire.

5. Season to taste with salt, pepper and lemon.

Alaçatı

Sour Cherry Dolmades

50–60 brined vine leaves
⅓ cup (80 ml) extra virgin
   olive oil, plus 2 tbsp
1 red onion, finely diced
2 garlic cloves, finely chopped
1 cup (205 g) red lentils,
   soaked in water
1 cup (175 g) bulgur, soaked
   in water
1 tbsp Turkish sweet red
   pepper paste (biber salcasi;
   available from Middle
   Eastern grocers)
1 x 400 g can crushed
   tomatoes
¼ cup (40 g) dried sour
   cherries, finely chopped
½ cup (20–30 g) finely
   chopped mixed dill, mint,
   parsley and spring onion
   (scallion)
2 tbsp pomegranate
   molasses
juice of 2 lemons
4–5 cups (1–1.25 litres)
   gently salted water or
   vegetable stock

flake salt and freshly ground
   black pepper to taste

1. Drain and rinse the vine leaves. You will need to cut the stalks off them if they are still attached, as they are fibrous and won't break down as you cook them.

2. In a large, heavy frying pan over medium heat, add the ⅓ cup (80 ml) of olive oil and cook the onion until soft, about 10 minutes. Add the garlic and sauté until aromatic, around 30 seconds.

3. Add the red lentils and bulgur and stir, coating everything in oil, then add your red pepper paste. Fry this until it is distributed through the mixture evenly.

4. Take off the heat and add your tomato, sour cherries, mixed greens and pomegranate molasses. Then season with salt and pepper.

5. Separate out the vine leaves that are too small or too irregular to roll and use them to line the bottom of a medium-sized saucepan.

6. Lay the leaves vein-side up in rows on a work surface. Place 1 teaspoon of the mixture in the centre bottom of the leaf. Fold the left and right sides over the filling and roll up, gently but tightly, from bottom to top. Place the leaf seam-side down in the saucepan so it doesn't unravel.

7. Repeat with remaining stuffing and leaves. Weigh the leaves down with a plate, and pour over the remaining olive oil, lemon juice and enough water or stock so that the edges of the plate are partially submerged. I don't salt this liquid as generously as I do for the stuffed capsicums on page 137. Generally, I find brined leaves quite salty to cook with, so keep that in mind.

8. Cover the pot and cook over low heat for about 35 minutes, or until leaves and stuffing are tender.

9. Once cooked, take off the heat and allow to cool while still covered with the plate. If you take the plate off too soon the vine leaves will discolour. Serve once cooled or store in the fridge doused with more olive oil.

Alaçatı

Artichokes with Broad Beans and Peas

This is my favourite way to cook artichokes. The ratio of water to vinegar is 3:1 and you can use white wine vinegar if you don't have any red on hand. You can keep these artichokes under oil if you completely dry them out after blanching them. Just arrange them standing, cut-side down, on a tray covered with a clean tea towel. When they're dry, pour a few tablespoons of olive oil in the bottom of a sterilised jar, fill it with artichokes and then cover them in olive oil. They'll keep in the fridge for months and you can pull them out and fry them whenever you need.

Serves 6 as a side

3 lemons
1 kg (2 lb 4 oz) baby artichokes
500 ml (17 fl oz) red wine
   vinegar, plus 3 tbsp
   for garnish
½ bunch thyme
1 orange
2 cloves garlic, sliced
400 g (14 oz) podded broad
   beans, or 800 g (1 lb 12 oz)
   unpodded
200 g (7 oz) podded peas,
   or 350 g (12 oz) unpodded
4 tbsp extra virgin olive oil
½ cup (10 g) torn mint

flaked salt and freshly ground
   black pepper to taste

1. Fill a large bowl with water, halve two of the lemons, squeeze the juice into the water, and add the lemon rinds into it too.

2. Clean the artichokes, removing the hardest outer leaves until you reach the heart of the artichoke, which has lighter and more tender leaves.

3. Cut the tip off the artichoke and trim the base. Rub the artichoke with half of the remaining lemon and plunge the cleaned artichoke heart into the bowl of water.

4. Add the 500 ml (17 fl oz) vinegar, thyme, juice and rind of one orange and the garlic to a pot with 1 litre (35 fl oz) of water, and season with salt and pepper. Bring to the boil over medium heat. Once it's boiling, add the artichokes.

5. Cook over medium–low heat for 15–25 minutes until the artichokes are soft and can be easily pierced with a knife, then drain.

6. Add the broad beans to a saucepan of boiling water and blanch until tender. This shouldn't take long at all; if fresh, the broad beans may only take a minute. Drain and refresh under cold water then peel (if unpodded) and discard skins. Transfer to a large bowl.

7. Add the peas to a saucepan of boiling water and blanch until tender; this will only take a minute. Drain and refresh under cold water then add to the bowl with the broad beans.

8. Add the artichokes and then season the mix with vinegar, olive oil, salt and pepper. Stir through mint close to serving.

Alaçatı

Sprouts with Walnut Skordalia

This skordalia is made with bread instead of potato and walnuts instead of almonds. I love the potato version, but I prefer this version with sprouts. If you want to use almonds instead of walnuts, use blanched ones.

Serves 4 as a side

750 g (1 lb 10 oz) brussels
    sprouts
¼ cup (60 ml) extra virgin
    olive oil
Aleppo pepper
100 g (3½ oz) stale bread
2 cloves garlic
200 g (7 oz) walnuts, roasted
    and shelled
1 tbsp red wine vinegar
dill to garnish

flaked salt and freshly ground
    black pepper to taste

1. Preheat the oven to 200°C (400°F).

2. Prepare the brussels sprouts by trimming the bottoms off them and then cutting them in half.

3. Marinate in a tablespoon of the olive oil, season with salt, pepper and Aleppo pepper and roast in a baking tray in the oven. They should be very, very golden brown by the time they're done, which will take around half an hour.

4. Take the bread and soak it quickly in water. Squeeze out the excess water and place the bread in a food processor.

5. Add the garlic, walnuts, red wine vinegar and remaining olive oil and blend until it forms a paste.

6. Add salt and pepper to taste, and extra water if needed.

7. Spread a layer of the skordalia on a plate and then top with the roast brussels sprouts. Garnish with extra Aleppo pepper and dill.

Gigantes with Pekmez and Orange

You can buy pekmez—grape molasses—from Middle Eastern grocers. I use it to sweeten dishes instead of using sugar as it's just grape juice cooked down. It's common in both Greek and Turkish cuisine. It differs from pomegranate molasses as it's not sour, though, so don't try and substitute one for the other.

Serves 6 as a side

500 g (1 lb 2 oz) dried lima beans or butter beans, soaked overnight
¼ cup (60 ml) extra virgin olive oil, plus extra to drizzle
1 red onion, diced
2 garlic cloves, sliced
¼ cup (60 ml) pekmez
½ bunch of fresh thyme
2 oranges
a few sprigs of marjoram, dill or mint to garnish

flaked salt and freshly ground black pepper to taste

1. Make sure you've soaked your beans overnight or for at least 12 hours. This will help them to cook evenly.

2. Preheat your oven to 180°C (350°F).

3. Drain the beans and place in a big pot covered in around 3 litres of water. I salt the water well and add a drizzle of olive oil in with the cooking water. I find this helps with the texture.

4. Bring up to a boil, then turn down to a simmer; the beans should take around 15–20 minutes to cook most of the way through. They'll get cooked again in the oven, so leave a little resistance. I cool my beans in the cooking liquid; I find this prevents them from drying out.

5. While the beans are cooking, start the base for the sauce. Sauté your onion in 2 tablespoons of olive oil until translucent, around 10 minutes, then add your garlic. Sauté for 30 seconds, then take off the heat.

6. Drain the beans once cooled—keep a bit of the cooking liquid on hand to add if the beans start to dry out during baking.

7. Put the drained beans in a baking dish and mix through the onion and garlic. Then add your pekmez, thyme, the grated zest from one orange and the juice from both of them, plus salt, pepper and remaining olive oil. Bake until you get nice crunchy, caramel bits on the tops of your beans; this should take around 20–30 minutes.

8. Pull out the thyme stalks, then check for seasoning and serve at room temperature garnished with fresh herbs.

Alaçatı

Black-Eyed Peas with Hazelnuts, Eggs and Honey

This sounds like a slightly odd salad, but its texture and flavour are really satisfying. It pairs well with my recipe for pickled sardines on page 95. Wild fennel also works well in this if you can get your hands on any, instead of dill.

Serves 4 as a side

400 g (14 oz) black-eyed peas, soaked overnight
100 g (3½ oz) hazelnuts
3 eggs
1 red onion, finely sliced
¼ cup (60 ml) red wine vinegar
1 cup (40–60 g) chopped mixed parsley, dill and spring onion (scallion)
¼ cup (60 ml) extra virgin olive oil
¼ cup (90 g) honey
1 clove garlic, minced
1 tsp cumin
a few sprigs of marjoram, leaves picked and finely chopped

flaked salt and freshly ground black pepper to taste

1. Soak the black-eyed peas overnight in plenty of water. This will reduce the cooking time and help the peas to cook more evenly.

2. The next day, in a large pot, combine the drained black-eyed peas with enough water to cover them. Bring to the boil and then reduce to a simmer. Cook uncovered until tender, drain and let cool.

3. Roast the hazelnuts in a preheated 160°C (315°F) oven until golden brown, and then allow them to cool before pulsing in a food processor to break them up slightly. You want them to be roughly in quarters: ground too finely, they won't give enough crunch to the dish.

4. Boil the eggs; for this dish, I prefer a semi-firm yolk so that they can be cut. Put the eggs into already boiling water for 6½ minutes and then take them out and let them cool slightly in their shells. Peel them and then dice into roughly 1½ cm (⅝ in) pieces.

5. Steep the onion in a little of the red wine vinegar for around 5 minutes, then start to combine the salad.

6. Stir the egg, onion, hazelnuts and mixed greens through the black-eyed peas. Then combine the olive oil, honey, garlic and remaining red wine vinegar with the cumin and pour over the salad. Garnish with the marjoram.

7. Check for seasoning and serve.

Alaçatı

Wheat Salad

This salad incorporates sweet, savoury and sour flavours to find balance. It works best in summer when stone fruits are abundant, but you can use whatever mix of fruit you like. Usually, I use nectarines, red grapes, plums and cherries—figs if it's later into summer. In winter, you can use citrus or dried fruit. I use isot, which is a Turkish chilli. Its flavour is very umami, slightly smoky and not very hot at all. So if you can't find it at a Middle Eastern grocer I would leave it out.

Serves 6 as a side

500 g (1 lb 2 oz) wheat grain
1 handful crushed pistachios
3 cups (500 g) chopped mixed fruit
2 cups (80–120 g) finely chopped mixed mint, dill, parsley and spring onion (scallion)
3 tbsp extra virgin olive oil
2 tbsp lemon juice
3 tbsp sherry vinegar
2 tbsp pomegranate molasses
100 g (3½ oz) feta, crumbled
1 large pinch of isot (Turkish chilli flakes)

flaked salt and freshly ground black pepper to taste

herbs to garnish (optional)

1. Soak your wheat overnight. This will help with reducing cooking time and will get a better texture in your grain.

2. The next day, in a large pot, combine the wheat with enough water to cover it. Bring to the boil and cook uncovered until tender, around 20 minutes. Drain and let cool.

3. Toast the pistachios in a preheated 160°C (315°F) oven for 10–15 minutes.

4. Place all ingredients in a large bowl, and toss to combine.

5. Check for seasoning and serve garnished with herbs.

Alaçatı

Potato Salad with Herbs and Roast Almonds

This potato salad is a super quick and super tasty addition to any meal that needs a starchy component. Dutch cream potatoes are my favourite with their waxy texture but you can use any potato you have on hand. The more floury potatoes will break up a little more after boiling, however. A good variation on this recipe is to take out the almonds and instead add sliced red onion and capers.

Serves 6 as a side

1 kg (2 lb 4 oz) Dutch
   cream potatoes
160 ml (5¼ fl oz) olive oil
4 tbsp red wine vinegar
2 lemons, juiced
1 clove garlic, minced
100 g (3½ oz) roast almonds
2 cups (80–120 g) chopped
   mixed chives, dill, mint,
   parsley and spring onion
   (scallion)

flaked salt and freshly ground
   black pepper to taste

1. Boil the potatoes with their skins on until very tender. Drain and peel off the skins while still warm.

2. Cut the potatoes up into rough chunks—I try to think of a mouthful size when I'm doing this.

3. Dress them in olive oil, red wine vinegar, lemon juice, garlic and a little salt. If you do this while the potatoes are still warm, they will absorb everything more easily. Leave to cool slightly.

4. Roughly pulse the almonds in a food processor. You still want them to have a crunchy texture, so don't take them too far.

5. Once the potatoes are a little cooler, stir through the mixed greens and almonds and check for seasoning.

Candied Grapefruit

"Spoon sweets" are fruits, and occasionally vegetables, that are preserved in syrup and served on a spoon, usually accompanied by a tall glass of cold water. This recipe is for grapefruit spoon sweets, which I eat as is or use baked into frangipane tarts.

2 large pink grapefruits
400 g (14 oz) caster sugar
1 cup (250 ml) water

1. Start by cutting the grapefruits in half horizontally. Then cut each half into eight wedges.

2. Place the grapefruit in a saucepan and cover with cold water.

3. Bring to the boil, drain and repeat blanching 6–8 times, until the peel no longer tastes bitter.

4. Then combine the blanched grapefruit, sugar and 1 cup (250 ml) water in a saucepan.

5. Cook over a very low heat, until most of the syrup has evaporated and the grapefruit tastes candied. This should take around 1½ hours.

6. Allow the grapefruit to cool in the syrup.

Alaçatı

3. Crete

They'd told me the best food in Greece was in Crete, that all the island's traditions had remained intact because it was the biggest one and people lived there all year round—not like the smaller islands, where people only stayed for summer. They'd told me there was lots of agriculture in Crete, because the climate was conducive to growing just about anything. Not just Greek vegetables—tomatoes, cucumbers—but tropical fruits, now, too—mangoes and avocados. They'd told me the plantations of oranges to make juice for the tourists were starving the island of its water supply.

If the best food in Greece was in Crete, then the best food in Crete was at Ntounias Slow Food. The restaurant was in a mountain village, Drakona, 40 minutes from the city of Chania. In the images I googled, the road leading there seemed to circle the face of a mountain, the village at its peak. It appeared that the tiered limestone of the surrounding mountains picked up light no matter the time of day.

The food at Ntounias was slow in every respect. Everything was grown on-site: cheese was made using milk from the animals they reared; an indigenous variety of wheat was grown to bake their bread; and they didn't use electricity to cook, only fire. In my research, I'd watched a YouTube video where the owner used traditional clay pots to fry potato chips in olive oil. Four pots had been presented in a row in front of the restaurant, raised in a wooden structure atop burning branches—they'd looked holy. In the video, Stelios, the owner, was wearing a white T-shirt smudged black with soot. He was doing his best to smile at the tourists filming as flames danced around him and oil splattered in the pan. I'd thought at the time that it looked like my kind of religion.

74—111

I'd tried to contact the restaurant for weeks with no reply. I sent emails and left voicemail messages. I'd even messaged their poorly moderated Facebook page; I could see they'd seen it. I booked a trip to Crete anyway, before the summer season started, with no real alternative plans to working there.

On my first night at a hostel in Chania, the owner, George, unravelled a map across his desk to circle local beaches, and I asked if he knew Ntounias. He said solemnly that the owners were some of his best friends in all the island.

George was well over six foot, and barely fit into the faded yellow Peugeot we drove to the restaurant the next morning. As it chugged and gasped its way up the mountain, his head poked out its broken sunroof and he spoke to me in a stage whisper about austerity measures in Greece. He wasn't a conspiracy theorist but stood on the edge of it. I reassured him that I hadn't come for money. My reasons for wanting to work at Ntounias were bigger than I knew how to explain to him, in the short time we had together on the drive. The expansive ideas I had about food and culture were bigger than I could explain to myself most of the time. I told him instead about the hand skills I was hoping to learn, about gardening, about finally learning Greek. He listened, nodding.

When we arrived, he relayed to the owners that I'd work for free in exchange for a room. I stood by awkwardly as he gave what looked to be an impassioned speech. They seemed perplexed. But they dragged my bags into the guesthouse anyway. I was working by the end of the day.

It wasn't just the food that was slow at the restaurant. The way they cooked was so unprocessed and unrefined that it was practically dysfunctional. On a windy day, the wait for olive oil-fried chips, cooked over the open fire, was over 40 minutes. With each salad ordered, we'd run out to the garden to frantically unearth onions and pick tomatoes, then run back to the kitchen with fistfuls of salad leaves and vegetables.

The restaurant was famous not just because of its approach but also because it served authentically Cretan food. Instead of feta in the Greek salad, Ntounias used *mizithra*, a fresh cheese like ricotta but made with goat's milk, making it more sour, and softer because of its higher fat content. Their *tzatziki* was so garlicky I couldn't eat it on an empty stomach. Their skillet pies were stuffed with cheese, fried, then doused in local honey. The island was covered in wild thyme, so the honey was spicy and herbaceous. I'd eat spoonfuls with my breakfast, snacking on the most quintessentially Greek things I could find, trying to ingest the culture. Stelios cooked with violent intensity, hurling rusks into the wood-fired oven to be baked. The rusks were nutty from the barley flour the restaurant grew and milled, and so hard they had to be soaked in olive oil before eating. Most days the restaurant was full by lunchtime, with everything sold out by three.

The other worker in the kitchen, Poppy, only spoke to me in simple Greek. Sternly watching my face, she repeated phrases slowly and forcefully. The intensity with which she spoke to me grew the more important the task at hand. But the harder she tried, the more I'd panic. My head would fill with white noise as she spoke at me. Occasionally I understood her without knowing how. Greek words were stored so deep in my subconscious that I'd be able to reply, but then they would disappear as if I'd said them in a dream. Now and then, I'd feel sure I knew the meaning of something, but when I'd turn to examine it, it would float just out of reach. Poppy watched me in those moments, frowning, shocked at my ability to respond sometimes but not always, to know words some days and not others. I was as confused as she was, I wanted to tell her. But of course, I couldn't. And this made her treat me with a particular type of suspicion.

I mostly relied on gestures and body language to get me through the workday. As she demonstrated the step-by-step of preparations, I'd fill the gaps in communication with what I already knew about cooking. She'd be relieved when I made things well, shaking her head and patting me on the back. She could dice an onion more finely in the palm of her hand than I could on a chopping board. And roll two dolmades at once. She got through her work much faster than I did, so she could sit out the front and have a beer before service.

Stelios tried to teach me Greek by holding up objects, shouting their names at me and getting me to repeat him. At first, I found it abrasive but soon it became a kind of game.

He was in charge of fire: the pots outside, the wood-fired oven inside. For six months over winter, he lived in the village alone with the animals. I saw it in everything he did. He didn't talk, more grunted when people approached him. Whirling through the kitchen he chewed on a tea towel he'd have tied around his neck. When he wanted help, he'd turn to me and give me a kind of prolonged blink—my cue to run to his side.

On my first night at Ntounias, and every night after that, when the restaurant closed we sat together at a table outside. We held up our glasses to any car that drove past, and they honked in reply. We drank *tsipouro*, which knocked me off my feet. But I didn't feel scared. The local radio played Cretan lute music in the background, and we sat without speaking. It was so perfectly still, the moon so luminous that it defied the darkness. Everything felt realer than real. The mountains seemed too vivid, humming in some sort of frequency I'd never experienced before. And the breeze felt like streams of silk rushing past my clothes. I felt so overcome by the physicality of that place that I wondered what it would mean for the rest of my life to come. I tried to take it in as much as I could, trying to cement it all in my memory so

I wouldn't lose the feeling. The feeling of everything being exactly as it should be: my feet on the ground, my body in the night. At home, a small part of me had always wished I was somewhere else, but in those moments at the table, I didn't long for anything. I'd read of people thinking they'd been permanently altered after being with particularly intoxicating people, and I wondered if that could happen with a landscape.

In the mornings, I'd open my door to catch the first morning light gleam through the field of greens. Sometimes I'd open the door a second time to check on the effect. I figured there was a particular hour that made it look most magic, with everything glittering true gold. But no matter the time, I was never less astounded by the beauty. I'd walk in the day with the two dogs from the restaurant, up the mountain and past the beehives, and I swore the air felt different in the light—more visceral, like the sun gave it weight, and I could wade through it, scoop it up with my hands. I tried capturing it in phone videos, but they came up so flat. But if I couldn't record it, was it real?

Stelios asked me why I kept walking and I wondered if the beauty had worn off for him. Or if he'd even seen it to begin with. I never told him I was testing my connection to the land, pressing my palms to the hot ground and feeling the rocks from the mountain to see if they gave me anything back. The landscape strangely reminded me of home. It was wild with its gnarled olive trees that twisted in on themselves, its palette of muted greens. My grandparents came from a mountain village near Thessaloniki, which I imagined looked similar. It was impossible to separate these feelings, or to be sure where they were coming from. What was it? Greek roots and belonging to the soil? Or because it reminded me of Australia but wasn't—a similar landscape without the same complications? Or was I only finding it beautiful because I was giving it time and paying it attention?

When I wasn't in the kitchen, I was in the garden with Stelios. He planted things by throwing handfuls of seeds into open fields, which made harvesting hard. We'd have to wade through thigh-high nettle to pick broad beans in the stinging sun. We seemed to be able to talk about the biggest things without words in those moments. He would turn to me and say, "Ella," shaking his head, squinting. "Money?"

And I'd shake my head. That wasn't what I was there for.

"Bravo, Ella," he'd say. "Bravo."

We'd take our knives into the fields and collect *horta*— Greek for wild, edible weeds—into plastic bags. The wild foraged greens were different in each region and totally dependent on season: blanched, served cold and slathered in olive oil, garlic and lemon. *Vlita*, a more robust spinach with purple-veined leaves, was just about the only green that grew in the summer sun.

But the *vlita* started to disappear as autumn rolled in and the crowds died down, and I realised there wouldn't be any use for me in the off-season. Once the novelty of the language barrier had worn off too, things started to weigh on me differently. The gap between cultures looked less like a river I could wade through and more like a chasm I couldn't climb out of. The more Greek I learnt, the more I realised I didn't know. And it was so slow, the learning.

On my walks, I obsessively planned for summers I could return. But I wanted more than summer. I wanted it to be my whole life. As I walked through the mountains where I'd felt hyper-connected, I suddenly felt detached, my body pre-empting my leaving. I was back to being untethered, rudderless.

Fava with Pickled Shallots

Greek fava is made from yellow split peas. Confusingly, in Turkey it's made from fava beans, as you would expect by its name. Somehow, at some point, it evolved when it was introduced to Greece. Now each country has its own version that it swears is totally different from the other. This recipe is for the Greek version, with the yellow split peas giving it a quite neutral but sweet and earthy taste that pairs well with salty or strong flavours. It's eaten traditionally as a meze, or to accompany proteins. Anyone who's been to Greece will have fond memories of eating fava with octopus on an island.

This fava is excellent with crunchy toast on the side, and even better with Cretan barley rusks, if you can get your hands on some.

Serves 6

For the fava:
2 cups (440 g) yellow
   split peas
2 brown onions, diced
½ cup (125 ml) extra virgin
   olive oil
1 carrot, diced
2 bay leaves
2 sprigs thyme

salt and pepper to taste

For the garnish:
4 shallots, sliced
¼ cup (60 ml) red
   wine vinegar
capers

1. Soak the split peas overnight in around 1 litre (35 fl oz) of water.

2. In a large saucepan, fry off the onion in 2 tablespoons of the olive oil until golden—around 15–20 minutes—then add the carrot and sauté until tender: another 15–20 minutes.

3. Add the drained split peas, bay leaves and thyme and cover with 1 litre (35 fl oz) of water.

4. Bring to the boil, then reduce to a slow simmer, skimming regularly (the more you skim the scum off the surface, the sweeter your fava will be). Once the split peas start to break down, they'll start to stick to the bottom, so keep an eye on them and stir occasionally. Add water incrementally if it starts to dry out.

5. While the peas are cooking, pickle the sliced shallots by steeping them in red wine vinegar for a couple of hours.

6. When the split peas are totally cooked through, which should take around 45 minutes to an hour, and nearly all the water has evaporated, take them off the heat.

7. Allow to sit and cool, then remove all the thyme and bay leaves. Purée until smooth, seasoning with the remainder of the olive oil and salt.

8. Serve the fava garnished with capers and shallots.

Crete

Pickled Sardines

These sardines are great as part of a summer meze spread next to lots of fresh tomatoes on toast. And they're also great atop fava (see page 93). Curing sardines in this way gives them a delicate texture. If the fish end up too soft for your liking, you can grill them slightly or flash them in a frypan.

Serves 6 as a side

500 g (1 lb 2 oz) sardines
 (I buy mine already
 cleaned and butterflied)
½ cup (125 ml) red
 wine vinegar
½ cup (125 ml) lemon juice
3 tbsp chopped parsley
1 tbsp chopped marjoram
 or thyme
2 cloves garlic, sliced
½ cup (125 ml) extra virgin
 olive oil

flake salt for seasoning

1. Make a layer of the butterflied sardines, skin-side down, in a baking dish or container that's not made of metal.

2. Mix vinegar, lemon juice and chopped herbs in a bowl.

3. Sprinkle sardines with salt, then with the lemon, vinegar and herb mix, to make sure the fish's flesh is covered. Start to distribute garlic slices throughout the layer too.

4. Create another layer of sardines, flesh down so that each sardine is sandwiched flesh to flesh with another.

5. Repeat until you have used all the sardines, using the aromatics, vinegar and lemon throughout the layers.

6. Once finished, top with olive oil. You want the olive oil to form a film over the sardines, protecting them from air. These will be ready in a few hours and can be kept for 4 days. They'll become firm once cured.

Sfakià Honey Pie

This pie is from the Sfakià region of Crete, which is renowned for its thyme-scented honey. Wild thyme grows rife throughout the island, so the honey that's produced is almost spicy in how herbaceous it is. You can buy Greek honey from supermarkets, but to imitate the flavour I put thyme or marjoram in the cheese mix and use lots of black pepper. Best eaten hot out of the pan.

For the dough:
500 g (1 lb 2 oz) plain (all-purpose) flour
270 ml (9½ fl oz) lukewarm water
2 tbsp extra virgin olive oil
2 tbsp white wine vinegar
1 tsp flake salt

For the filling:
100 g (3½ oz) kefalograviera, grated
200 g (7 oz) ricotta
a few sprigs of thyme or marjoram, chopped finely, plus more for garnish
2 tbsp extra virgin olive oil

flake salt and freshly ground black pepper to taste

good-quality honey to drizzle on top

1. For the dough, place all the ingredients in your mixer's bowl and mix with the dough hook for 5 minutes. The dough should be smooth, elastic and relatively soft. Add a little extra water if necessary, or flour if the dough is too sticky. This can also be done easily by hand.

2. Cover the dough with cling wrap and let it rest for half an hour in the fridge.

3. Divide the dough into 10 equal little balls.

4. Drain the cheeses of excess water and mix with the rest of the filling ingredients.

5. Roll each ball of dough into a round disc about 10–15 cm (4–6 in). You can choose how big you want to make these pies; I usually measure and cut them by tracing around a side plate so that they're easily fried in a pan. The dough should be rolled out to about ½ cm (¼ in) in thickness. Too thick, and the pies won't cook through; too thin, and they'll tear.

6. Put a glob of cheese mix in the centre of one round of dough and spread out evenly, leaving enough room around the edges to seal the pie. Don't use too much mix or, again, the pie will be too thick to cook.

7. Use water to dampen around the edge of the pastry round, then put another piece of pastry on top.

8. Press the pastry down to get rid of air bubbles before sealing the pie. I do this with a fork, pressing down the whole way around its edges to seal them.

9. Place each pie in a non-stick pan with a splash of olive oil and cook over medium–low heat for around 5 minutes per side. They should be crispy, caramel brown, and the pastry should be cooked through.

10. Serve warm with honey drizzled over them. Garnish with extra marjoram.

Crete

Horta with Lemon Potatoes

In Greece, horta is the blanket name for any seasonal edible weed. Each region prides itself on its own varieties of these greens—the harder to forage, the more prized. At tavernas, order a plate of horta and you'll receive a mix of whatever's growing at the time, blanched, served at room temperature, dressed in lemon, olive oil and garlic. It's my favourite thing to eat. I've used amaranth in this recipe, but you can substitute it for any green you have in your fridge: kale, silverbeet, English spinach. Just blanch them until tender.

Serves 6 as a side

1 kg (2 lb 4 oz) Dutch
   cream potatoes
1 bunch amaranth
¼ cup (60 ml) lemon juice
½ cup (125 ml) olive oil
2 cloves garlic, grated

flake salt and freshly ground
   black pepper to taste

1. Start by putting the potatoes on to boil. I leave the skins on, so they don't get waterlogged. Cook until very tender, then drain. Try to peel them while still hot.

2. Bring a separate pot of salted water up to boil and blanch the amaranth until tender.

3. Refresh the greens by plunging them into cold water to prevent them from overcooking, then drain.

4. Cut the potatoes up into bite-sized chunks and dress while still warm with the lemon juice, olive oil and garlic. I find the temperature helps them absorb the flavours.

5. Add the greens to the potatoes and mix well, making sure everything is adequately seasoned.

6. Serve at room temperature.

Trahana-Stuffed Tomatoes

Trahana is a type of cracked wheat that's been soaked in fermented milk and then dried out. Initially, making trahana was a way of preserving milk when there was excess production in spring and summer, but now it's made just because it's so delicious. Although it sounds intense, the flavour's not overpowering; it's got a comforting nutty, sour flavour. I use it here to stuff tomatoes; this recipe is best eaten on the day as sometimes the trahana dries. If you can't find trahana you can use a different grain like bulgur.

Serves 6

12 medium tomatoes,
  ripe but firm
1 red onion, diced
1 cup (250 ml) olive oil
2 cloves garlic, sliced
1 cup (180 g) trahana
1 cup (40–60 g) chopped
  mixed parsley, dill and mint
4 spring onions, sliced
¼ cup (60 ml) lemon juice
100 g (3½ oz) feta, crumbled

flake salt and freshly ground
  black pepper to taste

garlic yoghurt to serve

1. Start off by preheating your oven to about 160°C (315°F). You don't want the temperature to be too hot, or your tomatoes will split when you bake them.

2. Cut the tops off your tomatoes, but don't throw them away. Then use a teaspoon to hollow out their insides. You'll use this pulp in your filling mix; either run a knife through it to chop it into fine pieces or sometimes I grate the coarser bits. Set to one side.

3. In a saucepan, sauté your onion in a splash of olive oil until translucent. Then add and sauté off your garlic until it becomes aromatic, around 30 seconds.

4. Add the trahana and tomato pulp and cook this out. The trahana will absorb lots of liquid: if the mix starts to get dry before the grain is cooked, add olive oil or water. You want to cook the grain until it has stopped absorbing liquid. It should take around 20 minutes but keep tasting until the grain is soft.

5. Once it's finished, take off the heat and stir in your chopped herbs, spring onion, lemon, feta and seasoning.

6. Stuff your tomatoes until full—the grain shouldn't expand too much more but will a little. Put their little hats on and bake until their skin is puckered, for about 20 minutes. The longer you cook the tomatoes, the sweeter they'll taste, so if you have time, you could even put down the temperature and bake them for longer. I serve these at room temperature with garlic yoghurt on the side.

Crete

Village Salad

This is a pretty simple Greek salad; what makes it unique are the barley rusks. Paximadia are made all through Greece. Loaves of bread are cooked a second time, drying them into rusks. These rusks get crumbled through salads or eaten with cheese. My great-grandmother used to eat paximadia soaked in water—because they're so hard—and with only raw garlic to accompany them. When we were kids, we thought she was a witch because she also ate stinging nettles that would leave us covered in a rash. She lived to 106; I always thought she would live forever. I soak mine in olive oil and vinegar to soften them. And I prefer the Cretan variety, made of pure barley flour, but use any you can find. You can also substitute rusks for simple croutons.

Serves 4 as a side

4 tomatoes
2 Lebanese (short) cucumbers
½ red onion
100 g (3½ oz) feta
4 barley rusks, broken into bite-sized pieces
2 cups (80 g) loosely packed picked purslane

For the dressing:
¼ cup (60 ml) olive oil
2 tbsp balsamic reduction
1 tbsp pomegranate molasses
1 tbsp red wine vinegar
1 clove garlic, sliced

flake salt and freshly ground black pepper to taste

1. Start by making the dressing. Combine ingredients in a bowl, and leave for an hour or so to let the garlic steep.

2. Then cut your tomatoes and cucumbers into similar-sized pieces. I cut my tomatoes into eighths. My cucumbers I cut on the diagonal, turning the cucumber as I go to form triangle-ish pieces.

3. Slice the red onion as thinly as possible and add. Then crumble in the feta and rusks and add the purslane.

4. Douse in dressing and leave to sit for 5 minutes before serving to allow the rusks to soften.

Crete

Briam

In Crete, this vegetable bake is made in summer when eggplant (aubergines) and zucchini (courgettes) are plentiful and at their best. It might sound simple, but it is an exceptionally moreish dish. The sauce is heavy with tomato paste and caramelises when baked, and the excess olive oil gets flavoured from the vegetables and pools at the bottom of the baking dish, which is perfect for dipping bread. Serve briam warm or at room temperature. Great as a side or on toast for days after.

Serves 6

For the sauce:
1 red onion, diced
1 tbsp extra virgin olive oil
2 garlic cloves, finely sliced
1 cup (250 g) tomato paste
   (concentrated purée)
1 x 400 g (14 oz) can
   diced tomatoes
2 tbsp red wine vinegar
1 cup (250 ml) water
a few sprigs of marjoram
   or thyme, chopped

For the bake:
500 g (1 lb 2 oz) Dutch
   cream potatoes
500 g (1 lb 2 oz) eggplant
   (aubergines)
500 g (1 lb 2 oz) zucchini
   (courgettes)
a few sprigs of marjoram,
   thyme or dried oregano
½ cup (125 ml) extra virgin
   olive oil

flake salt and freshly ground
   black pepper to taste

1. For the sauce, start by sautéing the onion in the olive oil in a saucepan for around 15 minutes until translucent, then add the garlic and sauté until aromatic: 30 seconds.

2. Stir in the tomato paste and sauté for around a minute.

3. Pour in the can of tomatoes, red wine vinegar and water.

4. Bring to the boil then turn down to a simmer. Cook until most of the liquid has evaporated and the sauce has come together: around 15 minutes.

5. Stir in the herbs and check for seasoning.

6. For the bake, preheat your oven to 180°C (350°F). Peel and slice the potatoes into 1 cm (½ inch) rounds. Peel the eggplant lengthways in stripes, leaving 2-cm (¾-inch) strips of skin in between, then cut into 1 cm (½ inch) rounds. Slice the zucchini into 1 cm (½ inch) rounds. Transfer to separate trays lined with baking paper.

7. Season the vegetables with the herbs and salt, and douse them with the olive oil.

8. Bake the vegetables for about 25 minutes or until golden. Don't overcrowd the trays, or the vegetables will steam and get no colour.

9. Layer the browned vegetables in a baking dish. I start with potato, then zucchini, then eggplant, arranging them like tiles.

10. Cover the vegetables with the tomato sauce, then bake for around 40 minutes or until the tomato sauce has dried out and thickened, and has some colour on it.

Octopus Cooked in Red Wine

Octopus is one of the rare foods that benefits from being frozen: it helps to tenderise the meat. In Greece, octopus gets hung to dry in the sun, which is supposed to produce the same effect. Ask your fishmonger if your octopus has been tenderised or frozen—it makes all the difference.

For the octopus:
1 kg (2 lb 4 oz) octopus, cleaned
2 cups (500 ml) red wine
a few sprigs of thyme
¼ cup (60 ml) extra virgin olive oil
2 cloves garlic, sliced
4 tbsp red wine vinegar

For the marinade:
4 tbsp lemon juice
2 tbsp red wine vinegar
¼ cup (60 ml) olive oil
a few sprigs of marjoram or thyme, chopped
2 cloves garlic, sliced

flake salt

1. Place the octopus in a saucepan with the wine, thyme, oil, garlic and vinegar. Bring to the boil, then reduce to a low simmer. The octopus should sit below the surface of the liquid; weigh it down with a plate to submerge if you need. Cook for around 40 minutes or until tender. Remove from heat and allow to cool in cooking liquid.

2. Drain octopus.

3. Whisk the marinade ingredients together in a small bowl.

4. Depending on how you'd like to serve the octopus, you can either cut it into bite-sized pieces, toss it in the marinade and serve it cold, or, cut it into bigger pieces and flash it on a BBQ before marinating it and serve it warm.

Crete

Baked Okra in Tomato

I know many people have an aversion to okra because of its texture, but in this recipe, soaking it in vinegar prevents it from getting slimy.

Serves 4 as a side

700 g (1 lb 9 oz) okra
5 tbsp red wine vinegar
2 red onions, diced
5 tbsp extra virgin olive oil
4 cloves garlic, sliced
6 tbsp tomato paste
  (concentrated purée)
3 x 400 g (14 oz) cans
  crushed tomatoes
1 cup (250 ml) water
½ cup (25 g) chopped mint
½ cup (30 g) chopped dill

flake salt, freshly ground black
  pepper and lemon to taste

1. Cut the stems off the okra, and cut them in half on a diagonal if they are too large. Place in a baking dish.

2. Turn on the oven to 180°C (350°F). Coat the okra in 3 tablespoons of the red wine vinegar and put in the oven for about 15 minutes while the oven is heating up. In Greece, the okra gets left in the sun to absorb the vinegar. You just want them to warm through.

3. In a saucepan, sauté the onion in 3 tablespoons of the olive oil until translucent, around 15–20 minutes, then stir through the garlic.

4. Add the tomato paste, frying it off for around 3 minutes before adding the canned tomatoes, the remaining 2 tablespoons of red wine vinegar and the water.

5. Simmer on a medium–low heat until the sauce has come together: around 20 minutes.

6. Pour the tomato sauce into the baking dish with the okra and stir to combine.

7. Bake for around 45 minutes, or until the okra has a slightly golden colour on top.

8. Remove from the oven and let cool slightly before stirring through fresh herbs, and season with the remaining olive oil, salt, pepper and lemon.

9. Serve warm or at room temperature.

Crete

Baked Snapper

My favourite way to cook snapper. Super simple and super-fast. You can use the same recipe with any fish by adjusting the cooking time. Depending on how big your fish is, I'd serve one baby snapper between two to four people.

1 baby snapper, gutted
   and descaled
extra virgin olive oil
1 red onion, sliced
1 bunch marjoram or thyme
1 lemon, sliced into rounds
2 cups (500 ml) dry white wine

flake salt and freshly ground
   black pepper to taste

1. Preheat your oven to 180°C (350°F). Lay your fish into a baking dish. Rub olive oil over its skin, seasoning it with salt and pepper, too.

2. Stuff the onion inside your fish, also scattering around your tray. Do the same with the herbs and lemon.

3. Pour the wine into the bottom of the baking dish and pop in the oven for around 20 minutes or until your fish is just cooked through.

4. Squeeze some of the baked lemon rounds over the fish to serve, and garnish with extra olive oil and salt.

Melomakarona

These are some of my favourite Greek sweets because of their mix of savoury olive oil and herbaceous thyme honey. Instead of Greek thyme honey, you can heat some good-quality Australian honey with thyme to infuse it. These will keep in the fridge for a few weeks.

Makes about 25–30 biscuits

1½ cups (13 fl oz) olive oil
⅓ cup (75 g) white
   (granulated) sugar
1 cup (180 g) fine semolina
2 oranges, zested
⅔ cup (5½ fl oz) orange juice
½ tsp salt
1 tsp ground cloves
2 tsp ground cinnamon
2 tsp baking powder
½ cup (125 ml) Madeira
½ cup (55 g) ground walnuts
½ cup (50 g) almond meal
3½ cups (525 g) cake flour
   or plain (all-purpose) flour,
   or more as needed

For the honey syrup:
½ cup (110 g) white
   (granulated) sugar
1 cup (350 g) Greek
   thyme honey
1½ cups (375 ml) water
2 cups (250 g) walnuts,
   coarsely chopped

1. Preheat the oven to 180°C (350°F). Add the oil and sugar to a bowl and mix to combine.

2. Add the semolina, orange zest and juice, salt, cloves and cinnamon and roughly combine.

3. In a separate bowl, combine the baking powder and Madeira, then pour into the semolina mix, followed by the ground nuts.

4. Once that is all incorporated, start to gradually add in the flour, kneading to create a soft, oily dough.

5. Turn the dough out onto a working surface, adding a little more flour if it's too soft and difficult to shape.

6. Knead for 2–3 minutes, then cover and let rest for 20 minutes in the fridge.

7. Roll dough into golf ball-sized biscuits. Take your time doing this: if the biscuits aren't well formed they'll crack when baking.

8. Place the cookies about 4 cm (1½ in) apart on trays lined with baking paper and press a fork on the surface to create ridges.

9. Bake for about 25 minutes until the biscuits are golden brown and sound hollow when you tap them.

10. Meanwhile, make the syrup: in a medium saucepan, simmer the sugar, honey and water for 5 minutes and remove from the heat. Let cool.

11. Drop six to eight hot cookies at a time into the honey syrup and let them soak for about a minute—or a bit longer, depending on how soft or crunchy you'd like your melomakarona.

12. Once the biscuits have been soaked, sprinkle the crushed walnuts over them for garnish.

Crete

4. Home

Heat rises from the concrete slabs of my grandparents' driveway. I notice the smoke billowing off the spit halfway down Grantham Street. The smell hits me first, swirling around and engulfing me, giving me what I call *sore heart*—excessively warm feelings that ache.

It's my first Christmas back home and I'm greeted with a cheer as I turn into the backyard, always the last to arrive. They're all sitting on plastic chairs around a coffee table dragged out from inside, and bottles of VB are being shared between ornate crystal glasses that are glinting in the sun. Rebetiko is playing from the ancient radio in the kitchen, the sound scratchy, blown-out and perfect as it streams through lace curtains. Yiayia is offering around a plate of kefalograviera cut into tiny tiles, but suddenly she makes a beeline for me. I'm already in trouble. I'll have to be the best, best granddaughter to make up for the time passed. She calls me "κορίτσι μου"—my girl—holding my face in her hands, whispering it in my ear. It's the kind of affection I shy away from, ashamed of never knowing how to reciprocate.

I heard from my grandparents only twice while I was away. The first time was in Istanbul. When they called, the sound was distant and muddled, punctuated by directions being yelled out, half Greek, half English.

"Ella?" Yiayia said, "Where are you?"

"Istanbul, Yiayia," I said. "Turkey."

I heard Paupou from somewhere in the background: "Constantinople, Tourkía." Then, "We want you home, we want you here," and the conversation was over. The line was dead.

The second time, I received a letter from my grandfather that read:

112–151

Hi sweet hart,

How are you? I hope you have a good time in Peloponiso, specially in Mani. Watch this people theyar abit stabin some times. Your parents left yesterday they will meat Maddie then to Greece, wot days I don't know. Yiayia sent you her love, all so Kathy Grace Zoe and Veronica.

I keep all his notes in my diary. Birthday cards, Post-its.

Now everyone's safe together, here, under cherry trees encased in so much bird-proof netting they're almost impossible to identify. On the spit is an abundance of meat—chicken, lamb, pork, quails. Paupou's making a show of shaving the crunchy edges off as the spit turns, distributing the morsels delicately into eager hands with his tongs.

I go to stand next to him at the barbecue. He's circling it, giving himself different vantage points, crouching down to eye level, then hovering over to inspect it from above. The meat glistens, the fat forming droplets that hiss when they hit the coals. There's chicken salt on everything. Some additive in the salt makes everything crisp up and candy, turning everything an unnatural bright yellow. Paupou's wearing one of his button-up shirts that matches his eyes: glass blue. This daily uniform is designed to hide a prison-blue tattoo of a jaguar that runs the length of his right arm.

He says, "What do you think, Missy?" and turns to me, holding out a piece of meat. It's scorching hot. Saliva pools in my mouth as I try to chew, sucking in air and gnashing my teeth like a shark.

"Back home," he says, "they used to make only the fatty bits, the neck. And put so, so much salt on." He pretends to throw handfuls of salt at the meat. "It made everyone drink too, too much." His smile is reflected in his eyes. "Did you learn lots of yummy things over there?" he asks. I nod, my mouth stinging from salt.

"I started learning Greek, too," I say. He smiles as he turns back to the fire.

"What you wanna learn that for? We're in Australia now."

The dogs run past our feet, looping around the backyard and through the hole my grandfather cut in the fence that leads to Aunty Grace's.

Back under the cherry trees, my cousins are fighting:

"What do you mean he was blindsided?"

"You don't know what 'blindsided' means?"

"I know what it means, Veronica, I've just never watched *Survivor*."

Dad's holding out a drink to me, so I go to join them. He's the oldest of the siblings, *the golden son*. He's been in the background making cocktails, which aren't very traditional in our family but are starting to be because Dad needs something to be busy with in group situations. He gets too awkward, standing around. I have the same affliction. I think it's why I became a cook: to be at the party but have an excuse to be partially absent.

"Ella cooks with tarhana," Dad announces to the girls. "Yiayia makes it here, she dries it out on sheets. You don't have to go to the village. We have the village here," he says, raising two margaritas to the sky.

"You're the Greekest one now," Grace says as I sit down. "The Greekest Greek. Did you sort out your passport?"

"It was such an ordeal. I had to go to every office involved, one by one. And they all said they couldn't find my paperwork or pretended they couldn't speak English. I showed up at the police station every day just hoping they'd let me in."

I'd been trying to get my Greek passport for years. The Greek Embassy in Melbourne was open for about four hours a day, with no way of making an appointment. Their waiting room was a series of plush couches, all facing a TV that played Greek soap operas. Families congregated around the mock living room, looking angry or dismayed as the office workers smoked outside. Yiayia told me that I had to stay until they gave me exactly what I wanted. I'd taken her advice with me to Greece.

"Then, after days of getting nowhere, one morning, they processed it on the spot. Made it on a laminator, my European ID. It took five minutes." I shake my head. "Then the guy doing it said, 'Can I ask you something?' And I was so nervous."

I have this stupid tattoo on my hand that was supposed to be in allegiance to the Kurdish separatist movement, in some vague way. When I got to Greece, I found out it was an aggressive anti-establishment tattoo there. And I was in the middle of Exarchia: the most anarchistic area of Athens. Each day I wore a Band-Aid over it, though it kept falling off, so I'd try to clasp my hands together in a way that concealed it.

"I said, 'Sure', and all the cops turned to me. And then he said, 'Have you ever seen the show *MasterChef*? Do you know George Calombaris?' I nearly died from relief. I said, 'Yeah.' And he said, 'We love him! He was here. He came to Greece.'"

Greece had come full circle since my grandparents came over. When I was growing up, the Greeks in Greece said our family was stupid for leaving Greece to go to a country where everyone works so hard. But once the economic crisis hit, Australia was back to being the lucky country. And I was trying to complicate things by returning. They were watching me struggle against Greece—its bureaucracy, its economy—when it was what they'd walked away from.

Later, in the good room, we exchange gifts. There's a ponytail palm with a single rope of gold tinsel draped around it, leather couches covered in plastic, opulent glass swans, a chandelier. Veronica gets a bag she wants to exchange and tells everyone so. Paupou gets something to do with home maintenance, and

Yiayia's embarrassed about receiving anything. I get money because no one knows what I like, and Dad does too. We all get Tattslotto tickets and $50. Every time I go to my grandparents', a crisp note gets pushed into my pocket. My ex-boyfriend used to say giving someone $50 is how you say "I love you" in Greek. My card reads:

To our Grantdaughter

Ella have a wonderful Christmas sweet heart, Enjoy any thing you do. We hope that we have dinner all together next Christmas too.

They just want to keep me close and I'm flooded with that sore heart feeling. I look up and lock eyes with Dad, who's watching from the corner of the room. He smiles, gives me a slight nod and I'm embarrassed because I haven't been paying attention. I wonder why I run away from this unbounded type of love, searching for culture anywhere outside of this room.

Home

Chickpeas Baked with Lemon and Honey

This recipe is great for using up any left-over greens in your fridge. I use whatever I have—spinach, chard, sometimes beetroot leaves. Similarly, with the herbs, use a mix of whatever you have on hand.

Serves 4 as a side

1 bunch silverbeet
  (Swiss chard)
1 brown onion, sliced
¼ cup (60 ml) olive oil,
  plus extra to season
2 garlic cloves, sliced
2 x 400 g (14 oz) cans
  chickpeas, drained
2 tbsp honey
1 lemon
½ cup (20–30 g) chopped
  mixed dill, mint and
  spring onion (scallion)

flake salt and freshly ground
  black pepper to taste

1. Start off by preheating your oven to 180°C (350°F).

2. Wash the silverbeet – I finely chop it, then leave it to soak in a sink full of water before draining well.

3. Sauté the onion in 1 tablespoon of the olive oil in a saucepan for around 15 minutes until golden, then add the garlic and sauté until aromatic: 30 seconds.

4. Add the silverbeet and stir it through the oil, allowing it to wilt.

5. Add the chickpeas and sauté briefly.

6. Transfer everything to a baking dish and add the rest of the olive oil and the honey. Cut the lemon in half and add it to the baking dish.

7. Bake for around 40 minutes or until most of the liquid has been cooked out of the silverbeet.

8. Season with salt, pepper, extra olive oil and the pulp of the baked lemon. The lemon will be mellower than a fresh lemon, but taste as you go – it'll still be quite acidic.

9. Stir in the mixed greens and serve warm or at room temperature.

Home

Spanakopita with Homemade Filo

This pastry has a tendency to dry out a little, so be generous when brushing each filo layer with oil. It's best eaten straight out of the oven for the same reason. You can also buy pastry from the store, to make this recipe more quickly. If you want to try a different filling, we used to have leek pita, *prasopita*, growing up: sauté finely sliced leeks in a little olive oil and butter until tender, and stir through some dill.

Serves 6 as a side

For the pastry:
6½ cups (800 g) bread flour
1 pinch flaked salt
2 tbsp olive oil, plus extra
   to brush sheets
2 tbsp red or white
   wine vinegar
2 cups (500 ml) water
semolina to dust

For the filling:
½ bunch silverbeet
   (Swiss chard)
1 brown onion, sliced
3 tbsp olive oil
2 cloves garlic, sliced
1 cup (60 g) chopped dill
1 cup (20 g) mint, chopped
1 cup (120 g) chopped spring
   onion (scallion)
200 g (7 oz) feta
1 egg
1 lemon, juiced

flaked salt and freshly ground
   black pepper to taste

1. Preheat your oven to 180°C (350°F).

2. For the pastry: in a large bowl, add the flour and make a well. Add salt, olive oil and vinegar, then mix ingredients with your hands, gradually adding water as needed.

3. Knead the dough until it's smooth and elastic but not sticky. Add more flour if necessary.

4. Cut the dough into eight roughly equal-sized balls, and then cover and leave to rest for 20 minutes.

5. For the filling: start by preparing the silverbeet. Strip the green leaves off the stalks. Then, keeping them separate, slice both finely. Rinse, then drain.

6. Next, sauté the onion in a tablespoon of olive oil until golden: around 15 minutes.

7. Then add the garlic and sauté until aromatic, around 30 seconds, followed by the silverbeet stems, which will take about 10 minutes to cook through.

8. Then add in the silverbeet leaves, and sauté until just tender: 5 minutes.

9. Take off the heat to cool slightly before stirring through the dill, mint, spring onion, feta, egg, lemon juice and remaining oil. Mix and season well.

10. To roll out the pastry, press one ball of dough to flatten it as much as you can. With a rolling pin, roll out until the dough is approximately 1 cm (½ in) thick.

11. Now you can continue to use a rolling pin here to roll out your sheets; I use a pasta machine. Either way, you want your pastry to be around 2 mm (1/16 in) thick in the end.

12. Using a pasta machine: flour a work surface, then set the rollers to their widest setting and roll the pastry through the rollers.

13. Next, narrow the rollers by changing the machine setting by one notch, and pass the rolled pastry through the rollers again. Dust the pastry with semolina. Repeat the process until the pastry sheets have been passed through the narrowest setting on the machine.

14. Brush olive oil into a non-stick baking dish and sprinkle the bottom with semolina: this will prevent the bottom of the pie from getting soggy.

15. Lay one sheet of filo in the bottom of the dish, letting the edges overhang. Brush the pastry well with olive oil before laying down another sheet. Usually, I use four or so pieces on the bottom layer. I lay two pieces vertically across the baking tray and then two horizontally. Make sure to brush each layer with oil as you do so.

16. Add the filling, carefully spreading it evenly over the filo sheets. Then, make another layer of four pastry sheets on top, laying two pieces vertically and then two horizontally.

17. Holding the four corners of the overhanging filo, gently pull at each of the corners to remove a handful of the corner dough: this will ensure the corners are not too thick after they're baked.

18. Fold each edge over into the centre of the pie; they should fold neatly without too much overlapping. Pat down to remove any air pockets.

19. Brush the top with olive oil, and score your pie into serving-sized pieces with a sharp knife; this will help keep the pastry intact when you're cutting it later.

20. The pie will take about 45 minutes to cook (during this time, if the top is getting too browned, cover with foil so the insides can cook through).

Home

Gigantes with Tomato and Dill

These beans are one of the first things my Yiayia taught me to make. The most crucial element in this recipe is to be patient when cooking out your onions and capsicums before you add in the tomato. The longer you cook them out, the sweeter your result will be.

Serves 6 as a side

500 g (1 lb 2 oz) dried lima beans or butter beans
160 ml (5¼ fl oz) olive oil
6 sprigs fresh thyme
2 red onions, diced
2 garlic cloves, finely sliced
3 capsicums (peppers), thinly sliced lengthways
4 tbsp tomato paste (concentrated purée)
2 x 400 g (14 oz) cans diced tomatoes
3 lemons, juiced
½ cup (30 g) chopped dill

flaked salt and freshly ground black pepper to taste

1. Soak your beans in plenty of water overnight or for at least 12 hours; this will help them to cook evenly.

2. The next day, cover the beans with water in a pot. Salt the water generously and add 2 tablespoons of the olive oil and a few sprigs of thyme—I find the oil helps with the texture.

3. Bring up to a boil, then turn down to a simmer; the beans should take around 25 minutes to cook through. Make sure you cook them until they're creamy but not falling apart, as they'll get cooked a second time.

4. Once cooked, take them off the heat and allow them to cool in the cooking liquid (this prevents them from drying out).

5. While the beans are cooking, start your base for the sauce. Preheat your oven to 180°C (350°F). Sauté your onions in 2 tablespoons of the olive oil for around 15 minutes until they are translucent, then add your garlic.

6. Sauté your garlic for around 30 seconds, then add in your capsicums. Cook on a medium–low heat until they've lost a fair bit of their liquid and have started to caramelise. This will take about 15–20 minutes.

7. Add in your tomato paste, fry off for around 1 minute, then add your cans of tomatoes. Also add in a can full of water.

8. Simmer until the sauce has come together: around 20 minutes.

9. Drain your beans, leaving a little of their cooking liquid to one side in case you need it during the baking process.

10. Then mix the sauce through the beans in a baking dish, add in a few sprigs of thyme and bake until you get nice crunchy caramel bits on the tops, which will take around 20–30 minutes.

11. Once the beans are finished, let them cool slightly before seasoning with salt, pepper, lemon juice and the remaining olive oil. Stir through the dill now, too.

Home

Gemista—Stuffed Capsicums

This is the best method I've devised for making sure the filling of these capsicums is seasoned properly. Make sure your stock mix is quite bright from the lemon, and salty enough, or the rice will be flavourless. This rice filling can also be used to stuff dolmades. I soak my rice for a couple of hours before I use it, then drain it. This helps to keep the cooking time down.

Serves 5 as a light meal

6 red capsicums (peppers)

For the filling:
1 large red onion, diced
1 tbsp oil
2 tbsp tomato paste (concentrated purée)
1 x 400 g (14 oz) can crushed tomatoes
250 g (9 oz) arborio rice
50 g (1¾ oz) pine nuts, toasted
40 g (1½ oz) currants
1 cup (40–60 g) chopped mixed dill, mint and parsley
1 tbsp dried mint

For the stock mix:
400 ml (14 fl oz) chicken or vegetable stock
2 lemons, juiced
6 tbsp extra virgin olive oil

flaked salt to taste

To serve:
300 g (10½ oz) Greek yoghurt
1 garlic clove, peeled and crushed
flaked salt

1. Preheat the oven to 180°C (350°F).

2. Cut the top off each capsicum and clean out the stem, seeds and pith. Keep the top of the capsicum; you'll need it for the cooking process.

3. For the filling: sauté the onion in a frypan with 1 tablespoon of oil until translucent, then add in the tomato paste and briefly fry off.

4. Add in the can of tomatoes and simmer for around 5 minutes.

5. In a medium bowl, mix the tomato sauce with the rest of the filling ingredients. Stuff this mixture inside the capsicums. You want them to be relatively full, but keep in mind that the rice will swell once cooked.

6. For the stock mix: heat your stock in a separate saucepan and season it with lemon, salt and olive oil. The seasoning of this is integral as it will flavour the whole dish.

7. Arrange the capsicums in a baking dish, pour stock inside each one and pop on their lids.

8. Cover tightly with baking paper, then foil, and bake for 30 minutes or until the rice has absorbed the stock and is cooked through. Continue to add liquid during the baking process if they need it.

9. Remove the foil and baking paper and bake for 20 minutes more or until the capsicums are soft and browned on top, and the rice is cooked through.

10. In a small bowl, mix the yoghurt, garlic and salt until smooth, then set aside. Once the capsicums are done, leave them to rest until cooled, then serve with a spoonful of yoghurt.

Home

Trahana with Roman Beans

These beans remind me of lunches at my grandparents' house: lace tablecloths covered with a sheet of thick plastic for protection; plates of feta in the middle of the table and bread straight out of the oven. Great as a side, or good by themselves too.

Serves 6 as a side

1 kg (2 lb 4 oz) Roman beans
2 red onions, diced
½ cup (125 ml) olive oil
4 cloves garlic, sliced
3 tbsp tomato paste
  (concentrated purée)
1 cup (180 g) trahana
2 cups (500 ml) chicken or
  vegetable stock
2 x 400 g (14 oz) cans
  crushed tomatoes
½ cup (20–30 g) roughly
  chopped mixed dill and mint
1 lemon, juiced

flaked salt and freshly ground
  black pepper to taste

feta to serve

1. Start by peeling the Roman beans; because the sides of the beans can be fibrous, I peel them with a vegetable peeler. Top and tail them, then cut them in half on a slight diagonal.

2. In a saucepan, sauté the onion in 2 tablespoons oil until golden brown: around 15 minutes.

3. Add the garlic to the pan once the onions are done, and stir for around 30 seconds. Then add in the beans.

4. Stir the beans through the onion mix until they are coated in oil and have changed colour slightly.

5. Add the tomato paste into the pan, stirring until all the beans are coated.

6. Then add the trahana, also stirring until coated.

7. Add in half the stock and the canned tomatoes, and stir. Then bring up to a gentle simmer.

8. Check and stir every 5 minutes or so. Gradually add more stock when needed. You want the trahana to be cooked through and the beans to be tender. This will take around 25 minutes, depending on what type of trahana you use.

9. Once most of the liquid is absorbed and all elements are integrated and cooked, take off the heat to let cool slightly.

10. Stir through the herbs, lemon juice and remaining oil and check for seasoning.

11. Serve with feta on the side. These beans are even better the day after they're made.

Cabbage Rolls

I make these cabbage rolls with the same meat sauce that I use for moussaka. The sauce freezes really well so when you're making moussaka, I would recommend making one and a half times the recipe and keeping half to make cabbage rolls later. These rolls are better in the days after they've been made. If you have left-over cabbage leaves and rice mix you can slice and sauté the cabbage in a little oil, add the rice mix and make a pilaf.

Serves 6

1 cabbage
2 cups (440 g) arborio rice
½ cup (75 g) currants
1 cup (40–60 g) finely
    chopped mixed mint,
    parsley and dill
1 litre (35 fl oz) chicken stock
2 lemons, juiced
4 tbsp extra virgin olive oil

For the meat sauce:
1 brown onion, diced
2 tbsp extra virgin olive oil
2 cloves garlic, sliced
350 g (12 oz) lamb mince
2 tbsp tomato paste
    (concentrated purée)
½ cup (125 ml) dry red wine
1 x 400 g (14 oz) can diced
    tomatoes
1 quill cinnamon
2 bay leaves
1 orange, zested

flaked salt and freshly ground
    black pepper to taste

1. For the meat sauce: start by sautéing the onions in the olive oil in a saucepan for around 15 minutes until golden, then add in the garlic and sauté until aromatic: 30 seconds.

2. Stir in the mince, breaking it up with a wooden spoon, and sauté. Once it's all browned, add the tomato paste and fry off for around 1 minute.

3. Pour in the red wine to deglaze, and cook until evaporated.

4. Add the canned tomatoes, cinnamon, bay leaves and orange zest. Bring to the boil then turn down to a simmer. Cook out until most of the liquid has evaporated: around 30 minutes.

5. Meanwhile, to cook the cabbage, bring a large pot of salted water to a boil. Cut out the core of the cabbage and place the rest in the boiling water. As the leaves become tender they should fall away from the cabbage. You want them to be cooked enough that they are able to be rolled without snapping.

6. Take the cabbage leaves out of the water as they become tender, and place to one side to cool.

7. Mix your rice, currants and fresh herbs into the meat mix. Season with salt and pepper.

8. Take the cabbage leaves and categorise them into size. Big leaves will need to be cut in half; it's best if the vein of the leaf is removed as it's so thick it tends to take a long time to cook. Use any left-over bits of cabbage to line a saucepan that is deep enough to fit all your rolls in.

To serve:
300 g (10½ oz) Greek yoghurt
1 garlic clove, peeled and
    crushed
flaked salt

9. Take each leaf and spread flat. Place a heaped tablespoon of the rice mix down the end of the leaf closest to you, fold in the sides of the leaves and roll the cabbage leaf up.

10. Place the rolls in the pan, seam-side down. Repeat the rolling process with the remaining cabbage and filling, making sure all the rolls fit snugly together in the pan. If there are gaps around the rolls, fill them with extra leaves to prevent the rolls from opening while they are cooking.

11. Once all the mix is finished, weigh down your cabbage rolls with an upside-down plate.

12. Mix up your stock with lemon juice, olive oil and salt, check for seasoning and then pour over the rolls. Put the pan on the stove over medium heat. The liquid should come up just over the plate; top it up with water if it doesn't.

13. Bring to the boil then turn the heat down so they are cooking on a simmer. They should take around 40 minutes to an hour. They should be very tender, the rice totally cooked through. Once they're cooked, leave them to completely cool in the pan; this will help them keep their shape. Serve warm or at room temperature with garlic yoghurt.

Oxtail with Square Pastas

Hilopites, or "square pastas" as we called them as kids, are traditional Greek egg pasta. Growing up, we ate them cooked in rich chicken stock with butter, lemon and dill, which I would strongly recommend. But in this recipe, I cook them in the lemonato sauce I've cooked the oxtail in. If you can't find oxtail, you can use another cut of meat such as lamb neck or shank. I often use a lemonato sauce to braise chicken maryland.

Serves 4

750 g (1 lb 10 oz) oxtails
3 tbsp extra virgin olive oil
2 brown onions, sliced
2 cloves garlic, sliced
2 cups (17 fl oz) dry white wine
1½ litre (52 fl oz) chicken stock
½ bunch thyme
½ bunch marjoram
2 lemons
1 cup (200 g) hilopites

flaked salt and freshly ground
    black pepper to taste

1. Preheat your oven to 160°C (315°F).

2. Bring the oxtail out of the fridge and bring it up to room temperature before cooking.

3. In a casserole dish that can go in the oven, heat the olive oil over medium heat until very hot but not smoking, and brown the oxtails in batches. Get as much colour on them as possible: this is where the depth of your dish comes from. Remove oxtails as they're browned and set to one side.

4. In the same pot, add your sliced onions and sauté until golden brown: around 15 minutes.

5. Add in the garlic and sauté until aromatic—around 30 seconds—then deglaze with the white wine, cooking out until the wine has almost completely evaporated.

6. Add in the stock, herbs and oxtail. I squeeze the lemons, add in the juice and also throw in the fruit to be baked. Then cover with baking paper and a lid, transfer to the oven and bake until tender; this should take around 1½–2 hours.

7. Towards the end of the cooking process, once the meat begins to fall off the bone, I remove the herb stalks and the lemon rinds from the dish. I squeeze out the pulp from the fruit, adding it to the sauce.

8. Then you can either strain the sauce to remove the onion and garlic mix if you want the end product to be clearer, or leave all that in.

9. Next, add in your hilopites with 1 cup (250 ml) or so of water, if necessary, for the pasta to cook in. Then return to the oven to finish cooking.

10. Once the meat is tender and pasta is cooked through, check for seasoning and serve from the oven.

Chicken Souvlaki

When we make souvlaki at home, I serve the meat in yoghurt flatbreads and with tzatziki. Brining is the secret to cooking good chicken. Apart from helping to season the meat, it helps keep meat tender. You can use a 5% salt solution if you want to brine your chicken overnight. But I usually like to do it at just under 10% and have it done in a couple of hours. This recipe is for cooking chicken thighs on a spit, but the brine is suitable for any cut. I brine chicken breasts with the skin on in this same way, then sear the skin in a pan and roast them in the oven.

For the brine:
2 cups (500 ml) boiling water
180 g (6 oz) table salt
3 tbsp honey
1 bunch thyme
2 lemons, juiced
6 cups (1.5 litres) cold water

For souvlaki meat:
200 g (7 oz) chicken thigh
   per person
extra virgin olive oil
dried oregano
lemon juice

flaked salt and pepper
   to taste

1. To make the brine, put the boiling water in a saucepan or heatproof vessel and dissolve the salt and honey into it.

2. Then throw in the thyme, lemon juice and the cold water. Leave this mixture to cool completely; you don't want to put your chicken into hot brine, or it will start to cook. You can also cool your brine by putting it in the fridge if it's still warm.

3. Once it's cooled right down, immerse your chicken in it. The chicken needs to be fully covered by the liquid. Leave the chicken in the salt solution for 2 hours in the fridge.

4. Take your chicken out of your brine solution and pat dry.

5. Rub your chicken with olive oil, pepper and oregano. It should be pretty salty from the brine; I usually wait to add extra salt until it's cooked, and only after tasting.

6. I cook my chicken over a spit. Usually, when Dad and I cook a spit with chicken on it for around 20–30 people, it takes around 1½ hours over an open flame. But this time will vary greatly depending on how many people you're cooking for, and how hot your fire is. These chicken thighs are also great cooked straight on a barbecue.

7. Once the chicken is cooked through, season with lemon juice and salt if needed. Cut each thigh into four or five strips on a diagonal. Serve with flatbread and tzatziki, and a simple tomato salad.

Home

Steak Marinated in Red Wine Vinegar and Herbs

This isn't the Greekest recipe, but it's how I cook steak at home. The marinade should be enough for two steaks, so multiply it accordingly. But be generous with your estimation; it's great mopped up with bread.

1 porterhouse or scotch fillet steak—or whichever type of steak you prefer

For the marinade:
4 tbsp extra virgin olive oil, plus extra for oiling the steak
3 sprigs fresh oregano
3 sprigs marjoram
1 clove garlic, sliced
4 tbsp red wine vinegar

flaked salt and freshly ground black pepper to taste

1. Bring your steak to room temperature before cooking. Heat a grill pan, or cast-iron or heavy non-stick frying pan.

2. In a small dish that can fit the steak snugly, combine the extra virgin olive oil, salt, herbs, garlic and red wine vinegar.

3. On a separate plate, oil the steak lightly then put it in the hot pan and cook for around 3 minutes on each side. The cooking time will change depending on the size of your steak but I usually cook my steak rare for this dish.

4. Remove it and place it into the marinade dish, and rest it for 2 minutes on each side.

5. Remove the steeped steak to a board, cut it into thin slices on the diagonal and arrange on a serving dish. Pour the marinade over the steak and serve with bread.

Moussaka

Making moussaka is incredibly time-consuming but well worth the effort. I use coarsely minced lamb shoulder because I love the richness, but you can use beef mince if you find the flavour of lamb too strong.

Serves 8

1 kg (2 lb 4 oz) eggplants (aubergines)
½ cup (125 ml) extra virgin olive oil
1 kg (2 lb 4 oz) Dutch cream potatoes
½ cup (75 g) sesame seeds

flaked salt and freshly ground black pepper to taste

For the meat sauce:
2 brown onions, diced
3 tbsp extra virgin olive oil
3 cloves garlic, sliced
750 g (1 lb 10 oz) lamb mince
3 tbsp tomato paste (concentrated purée)
1 cup (250 ml) dry red wine
2 x 400 g (14 oz) cans diced tomatoes
1 quill cinnamon
2 bay leaves
1 orange, zested
½ cup (25 g) mint, finely chopped

For the béchamel sauce:
125 g (4½ oz) butter
125 g (4½ oz) plain flour
1 litre (35 fl oz) milk, warmed
2 eggs
150 g (5½ oz) kefalograviera, grated

flaked salt and freshly ground black pepper to taste

1. For the meat sauce: start by sautéing the onions in the olive oil in a saucepan for around 15 minutes until golden, then add in the garlic and sauté until aromatic: 30 seconds.

2. Stir in the mince, breaking it up with a wooden spoon, and sauté. Once it's all browned add the tomato paste and fry off for around 1 minute. Pour in the red wine to deglaze and cook out until evaporated.

3. Add the canned tomatoes, cinnamon, bay leaves and orange zest. Bring to the boil then turn down to a simmer. Cook until most of the liquid has evaporated: around 30 minutes. This sauce should be thicker than a bolognese, otherwise your moussaka won't hold together when sliced. Take off the heat and allow to cool slightly before stirring through the mint.

4. Preheat the oven to 180°C (350°F). Peel the eggplants in lengthwise strips, leaving 2-cm (¾-in) strips of skin in between. Then cut into rounds that are about 1½–2 cm (⅝–¾ in) thick.

5. Lightly salt the eggplant, douse in around ¼ cup (60 ml) oil and leave to one side for 5 or so minutes to marinate. Peel and slice the potatoes into 1 cm (½ in) rounds, and also marinate in ¼ cup (60 ml) oil for 5 minutes.

6. Place eggplant and potato on separate oven trays lined with baking paper and roast for 25 minutes, until golden brown.

7. For the béchamel: use a large saucepan to melt the butter over low–medium heat then add the flour, whisking continuously to make a paste. Pour in the warm milk in a steady stream, and continue to whisk until thickened.

8. Remove from the heat and quickly whisk in the eggs and kefalograviera to prevent the eggs from cooking. Season with salt to taste.

9. In a large baking dish, start by creating a layer of potatoes covering its base, followed by a layer of eggplant, then the meat sauce, spreading it out evenly. Top with the béchamel, smoothing it out evenly with a spatula. Then sprinkle with sesame seeds.

10. Bake for around 45–60 minutes or until its crust turns light golden brown. Allow to cool slightly before cutting into pieces.

Home

Galaktoboureko

My favourite dessert of all time.

Serves 10

250 g (9 oz) salted butter,
  for brushing the filo
1 packet of filo pastry

For the syrup:
550 g (1 lb 4 oz) caster sugar
450 ml (16 fl oz) water
rind from 1 lemon

For the custard:
400 ml (14 fl oz) single
  (pure) cream
600 ml (21 fl oz) milk
200 g (7 oz) caster sugar
1 tsp vanilla extract
150 g (5½ oz) fine semolina
150 g (5½ oz) salted butter
4 eggs

1. Preheat your oven to 165°C (325°F).

2. For the syrup: combine the sugar, water and lemon rind in a pot, place over medium heat and bring to the boil. Once the sugar has dissolved completely, set aside to cool.

3. For the custard: in a second pot, add the cream, milk, half the sugar and the vanilla. Place over a medium heat and bring to the boil.

4. As soon as the cream mix has come to the boil, whisk in the semolina. Do this incrementally: if you add too much at once your mix will get lumpy. Whisk until mix thickens: 5–7 minutes.

5. Once the mix has thickened, remove from the heat and add the butter. Continue whisking until the butter is completely incorporated and the mix has cooled slightly.

6. Beat the eggs in a mixer with the remaining caster sugar until white and fluffy.

7. Once the semolina mix is lukewarm, gently fold through the egg mix with a spatula.

8. Melt the butter for brushing the filo. Generously brush a baking dish with some of the melted butter then start assembling the pie by spreading sheets of filo in the dish and brushing with butter.

9. Repeat the process with half of the packet of filo, then spread the custard on top and fold over the filo that is hanging over the edges. Brush with butter.

10. Set one sheet of filo aside and add the remaining sheets over the custard, drizzling each one with melted butter. Then carefully cover with the final sheet, tucking it under the edges of the pie.

11. Score your pie into serving-sized pieces with a sharp knife; this will help keep the pastry intact when you're cutting it later. Then pour the remaining butter over the top and bake for around 1 hour or until golden and crunchy.

12. When ready, remove from oven and pour the cold syrup over the pie.

Acknowledgements

I'd firstly like to thank my family. The realisation of this book was a long process, and I couldn't have done it without the support of many people. I'd like to thank Kevin Högger for his beautiful design work, Jessica Grilli for her help with photos, Jane Willson and the team at Murdoch Books for bringing this edition into the world, and Pat Nourse for championing its first edition. I'm so proud of this book and the collective work it represents.

Index

Published in 2024 by Murdoch Books, an imprint of Allen & Unwin
First published in 2022 by Ella Mittas

Murdoch Books Australia
Cammeraygal Country
83 Alexander Street
Crows Nest NSW 2065
Phone: +61 (0)2 8425 0100
murdochbooks.com.au
info@murdochbooks.com.au

Murdoch Books UK
Ormond House
26–27 Boswell Street
London WC1N 3JZ
Phone: +44 (0) 20 8785 5995
murdochbooks.co.uk
info@murdochbooks.co.uk

For corporate orders and custom publishing, contact our business development team
at salesenquiries@murdochbooks.com.au

Publisher: Jane Willson
Editorial managers: Virginia Birch, Breanna Blundell
Design manager and cover designer: Megan Pigott
Designer: Kevin Högger
Design typesetter: Susanne Geppert
Photography assistant: Jessica Grilli
Production director: Lou Playfair

*Murdoch Books acknowledges the Traditional Owners of the Country on which we live and work.
We pay our respects to all Aboriginal and Torres Strait Islander Elders, past and present.*

ISBN 978 1 76150 017 6

 A catalogue record for this
book is available from the
National Library of Australia

A catalogue record for this book is available from the British Library

Colour reproduction by Splitting Image Colour Studio Pty Ltd, Wantirna, Victoria
Printed by 1010 Printing International Limited, China

OVEN GUIDE: These recipes were tested in a fan-forced oven. For conventional ovens, as a general rule,
set the oven temperature to 20°C (35°F) higher than indicated in the recipe. You may find cooking times
vary depending on the oven you are using.

TABLESPOON MEASURES: We have used 20 ml (4 teaspoon) tablespoon measures. If you are using
a 15 ml (3 teaspoon) tablespoon add an extra teaspoon of the ingredient for each tablespoon specified.

10 9 8 7 6 5 4 3 2 1